To Sim & Barbara ~
My last and best associate ~
and most distinguished colleague
and friend

הבנ/בב ה

Harold

I Will Not Let You Go Until You Bless Me

Memoirs of a Reform Rabbi

I Will Not Let You Go Until You Bless Me

Memoirs of a Reform Rabbi

Harold S. Silver

KTAV Publishing House, Inc.
Hoboken, New Jersey

Copyright© 2002
Harold S. Silver
Library of Congress Cataloging-in-Publication Data

Silver, Harold S.
I will not let you go until you bless me: memoirs of a reform rabbi/ by Harold S. Silver
    p. cm.
ISBN 0-88125-729-X
    1. Silver, Harold S. 2. Rabbis--Pennsylvania--Pittsburgh--Biography. 3.
Rabbis--Connecticut--West Hartford--Biography. 4. Reform Judaism--United States. 5.
Jews--United States--Biography. I Title.

BM744.S5415 A3 2002
296.8'341'092--dc21

2001050673

Distributed by
Ktav Publishing House, Inc.
900 Jefferson Street
Hoboken, NJ 07030
201-963-9524 FAX 201-963-0102
Email orders@ktav.com
Website www.ktav.com

To Ruth Lee

Transcendent co-partner in my life,
my profession and in all things
blissfully creative and fulfilling.

Table of Contents

Preface

In June of 1993, after having served in the American Reform rabbinate for forty-two years, I retired. For over four decades I was privileged to have served three great congregations. The first two were in the city and suburbs of Pittsburgh, Pennsylvania. From December 1951 through January 1955, I served as assistant and then associate rabbi at the historic Rodef Shalom Congregation under Rabbi Solomon B. Freehof. From 1955 until 1968, I served as rabbi of Pittsburgh's first suburban Reform congregation, Temple Emanuel of the South Hills in Mount Lebanon. In the spring of 1968, I was called to the pulpit of Congregation Beth Israel in West Hartford, Connecticut, succeeding Rabbi Abraham J. Feldman. For the next quarter of a century, as senior rabbi, I ministered to the fourteen hundred families who comprised the membership of Connecticut's oldest and largest New England Jewish congregation, founded in 1843.

While the rabbinate has no monopoly on career frustration, one enters my unique profession with a job description that defies human attainment. This is hinted at slyly, facetiously, and ominously during the five years of rabbinical training. Despite the admittedly limited student-pulpit experience, not to mention the periodic cautionary advice and horror stories shared with the rabbinical student body by faculty members and visiting rabbis from the field, it isn't until the post-ordination baptism by fire in the ongoing daily rabbinate that the fledgling rabbi comes to sense a shocking truth. What has been expected of him or her professionally and personally in measuring up to the basic rabbinical job description is utopian at best and unrealizable at worst.

Every rabbinical school graduate knows well beforehand that scholarship and teaching have historically constituted the primary role of the rabbinate—preaching and teaching in the pulpit, the classroom, the lectern, and the dais. What can never be fully imagined before entering the field is the awesome impact of the rival claims upon the modern-day rabbi, wherein preaching and teaching are forced to take a back seat to life-cycle priestly officiation, pastoral service in hospital, home, and study, marriage, divorce, and family counseling, institutional programming, conducting worship services, ambassadorial outreach to the non-Jewish community, and assuming in general the complex mantle of spiritual CEO. When you add to these public life duties and responsibilities the parallel personal commitment of the rabbi to his or her own marriage, family, and private life needs and pleasures, only then does the rabbi begin to seriously wonder how a congregation can harbor such superhuman expectations of its religious leader.

There is yet another career pressure that affects the rabbi even more negatively than the realization that it is impossible to satisfy all lay expectations. What chiefly flags rabbinical drive and spirit as the years go by is the constant unreal demand to shift one's emotional gears time and again as we wend our way on our professional rounds, spinning breathlessly from depressing to joyous life-cycle rituals— that is to say, from the grave to the wedding altar; from hospital deathbed vigils to joyous at-home blessings of thanksgiving for a screaming eight-day-old circumcised infant boy; from a premarital-conference mood of breathless adoration and starry-eyed anticipation to the embittered, recriminatory damnations of husbands and wives at each other's throats on the threshold of divorce; from shepherding an awestruck convert candidate through the final, moving declaration of accepting full Jewish status while holding one's breath in the explosive presence of the convert's non-Jewish parents and siblings, who more often than not are understandably consumed with suppressed and even overt feelings of resentment, anger, and guilt.

These are but a handful of the utterly unique and unending mixed emotional experiences that fracture a rabbi's daily life and create an unstoppable roller-coaster ride of emotional highs and lows that can tear any rabbi apart.

In the midst of my present retirement bliss, while my own career is still wondrously fresh and vivid in my mind, it is my fervent wish in this book to try and separate the gore from the glory in my incredible profession. My inner heart's desire is to have both rabbinical and lay leaders step back from their respective religious and secular roles in the synagogue and in the Jewish community. And, as they step back, my fervent hope is that both rabbis and laity will realistically redefine, restructure, and upgrade their oftentimes impossible and uncalled-for relationships with each other. By honestly reexamining how laity and clergy regard one other and treat one other, my deeper wish is that we can forge the kind of religious and secular ties that Judaism demands of us. If some of my rabbinical insights, analysis, and musings occasionally border on sarcasm or gallows humor, I apologize in advance. The three great congregations I have had the honor of serving for over four decades have been kind, patient, and forgiving enough to bear with my unique brand of pulpit and personal humor. For that, I am most grateful. I am indebted to Joyce Sturm, former temple religious school administrator and present Executive Director of Temple Sinai of Newington, Connecticut for her exemplary editorial assistance in producing this book.

West Hartford, Connecticut
October 2001

1

Not Going Gently into the Night
(or, How to Retire Gracefully and Painlessly)

I was lucky in my Rabbinical career. When it came time for my retirement I had two senior role models to draw upon for guidance and emulation—one majestic and the other madcap. The "majestic" role model was the Senior Rabbi with whom I began my career in 1951 as his Assistant. He ultimately eased into his retirement with effortless grace, dignity, and delight. He paved the way maturely and smoothly for his young successor to take over completely. He saw to it that any potential clash of Rabbinic egos between himself and his successor never occurred. They both made certain that the professional and personal do's and don'ts of retirement behavior were scrupulously understood, sensitively adhered to, and mutually agreed upon.

The "madcap" rabbinic retirement role model that I had to contend with had at least one great positive for me. It convinced me powerfully long before my own retirement that my successor would never have to put up with what I had to endure! I would like to think that even in the face of the depressing successor-emeritus which I had to live with in the first few years of my coming into my last congregation as senior rabbi, I would have instinctively paved the way spiritually and properly for my successor. To me, such successor-emeritus transitions in the rabbinical profession have always called for a retiring colleague to demonstrate to the successor

1

what we refer to in Jewish life as menschlikeit—character, sensitivity, and good manners. One would normally expect a rabbi, above all, to be acutely responsive to the delicate and sensitive matter of retirement etiquette. The sad reality, however, is that my profession generates some weird, inflammatory, and highly questionable behavior among too many of my older colleagues which I have found painfully distressing and disillusioning to deal with.

The biggest potential for successor-emeritus friction is the reluctance of far too many rabbis, immediately upon retiring, to steer totally clear of "womb-to-tomb" life-cycle officiation. It is, of course, highly ego-flattering to have your old members continue to call upon you in your retirement to officiate at yet another joyous or sad occasion in their family lives. ("You were there for me, Rabbi, when my mother died and when I had my by-pass operation; you were there at the birth of *all* of my children; you Bar Mitzvahed my kids; you inspired them on to Confirmation; you converted my son-in-law; you were there under the chuppah to unite my sons and daughters in marriage; you were an unforgettable part of our family life for two and three generations; we don't *know* the new rabbi like we know and love *you*; it can *never* be the same without you; we are certain that your successor will more than understand and step aside for you to officiate!")

What recently retired rabbi has not been subjected to this emotional litany and a host of other long-time member pleas to rerobe for yet another round of life-cycle officiation. Our colleagues, however, who succumb to these post-retirement invitations to officiate are, if truth be told, only opening up a can of worms for their successors. They are, in effect, shutting their successors out of the opportunity they once had when they first came to their new congregations and were expected to establish instant professional and personal relations of their own. Far too often, the retired rabbi unprofessionally, if not selfishly, forgets that at the beginning of his own tenure years and years ago as incoming senior rabbi, he, too, once eagerly desired to wade into the normal cycle of rabbinic officiation. Such life-cycle officiation is the normal, timely, and indispensable entrée into the lives and hearts of new members who stand waiting eagerly to get to know their new rabbi.

Obviously, there are occasional exceptions to the practice of retirees coming out of retirement to officiate. One's own family weddings, of course, are at the top of the list, as well as that tiny cadre of truly close personal friends many rabbis make in the congregation who over the years are truly like family. Any sensitive successor should bow out immediately and graciously from this type of officiation. However, for the rank-and-file member's simchah (joyous occasion) or tsurah (sorrowful event), retirement really should herald the natural and graceful end of officiation for the emeritus! And what is more important, the mature recognition that this career "finis" is the retiree's own *true* desire. If the congregant still wants to include the "old" rabbi, there is nothing in the world preventing the family from seeing to it that the retired rabbi is thoughtfully and lovingly added to the overall invitation list— where, for simhas, the retired rabbi can still be present at the event, but in the more proper retiree role as joyous celebrant and *not* as officiant. For sorrowful occasions, the retired rabbi can also choose to be present at the funeral and home visitation, but now more properly in the role of fellow mourner dutifully and comfortingly paying one's professional and personal respects along with all of the other mourners. There are also some occasions when it is more than fitting for the new rabbi to invite his predecessor to share the eulogy of a pillar-member of the congregation. The problem here is that if such unending co-officiation becomes the norm, then the successor will constantly feel "under the gun" to accede to this kind of co-officiation, never allowing the successor to go it alone once and for all! Truly letting go in this officiating area is the only practical and dignified key to a frictionless retirement.

Another area of potential friction, or really adjustment, for the retiree is to make a professionally proper decision as to where to sit in the sanctuary when coming to worship *after* one retires. Except for rare "state" occasions, the smart place to be is in a pew! After a career lifetime in the pulpit, conducting worship, preaching and teaching, and being the absolute, central focus of lay attention, it does take some psychological and emotional adjustment to be permanently out of the altar limelight. But a mature and healthy rabbinic ego should quickly come to sense that the pulpit spotlight now inevitably, properly, and totally belongs to the successor. Sitting in a pew, also, need never diminish the persona of the emeritus. The mantra to be vigorously repeated, if the emeritus is to adapt to serene retirement status in the congregation, is: "I have not been *replaced!* I have only been *succeeded!*" Equally effective and compellingly realistic is another mantra: "I am history now. As for the future, it belongs to my successor. " In other words, when it's over, it's over! If the first three mantras prove ineffective, one final mantra should do the trick: "Letting go is never easy. But hanging on is worse!"

The charm, pleasantness, and uniqueness of the emeritus in the pew is actually manyfold. In retirement, you finally have the delight of worshipping together with your spouse, who for a career has been missing from your side. Most spouses are joyously relieved to switch from the nervous role of rabbinic defender to the serenity and anonymity of simple congregational couple. For the emeritus, in fact, it is almost perverse fun just to sit back quietly in the pew and chuckle at, if not *revel* in, the inevitable comparisons that are being continually made, and which in more cases than not serve only to enhance one's emeritus stature. Perversity aside, which I know is most unrabbinical, it is simply humbling and yet invigorating to observe how one's successor goes about "your" rabbinate on or off the altar in a bracingly different but still positive, meaningful, welcome, and fulfilling manner.

2

Why Being a Rabbi Is No Job for a Nice Jewish Boy or Girl
(or, Confronting the Rabbi Shortage)

When I was ordained in 1951, the two campuses of the Hebrew Union College–Jewish Institute of Religion in Cincinnati and in New York averaged around forty ordinees each year. Even when women began to be ordained in Reform Judaism after 1972, the classes of men and women together still continued to average about forty. By the end of the twentieth century, however, women rabbinical students comprised close to 50 percent of the student body. The Cantorial School of the Reform movement, during the past several decades, has become almost totally female. The male chazzan (cantor) is fast becoming a disappearing synagogue professional in Reform Jewish life. The same situation will probably prevail in the Conservative movement within the next several decades. Only in Orthodox synagogues are they still rigidly holding the line against allowing women to serve in either the rabbinate or the cantorate.

The huge infusion of East European Jews into the once predominantly German-Jewish Reform congregations in the second half of the twentieth century more than tripled the number of Reform congregations since 1945 from 250 to over 900. About 200 of these congregations are substantially under a hundred families each. Because of their small size and remote small-town locations throughout the United States, these small congregations do not have full-time rabbis. Only when the High Holy Days annually occur is there a major effort by our Reform seminary to assign its rabbinical students to serve the High Holy Day needs of these far-flung minuscule Jewish communities. Of the remaining 700 congregations, there are at present about twenty-five of normal 200-family size or larger seeking to engage full-time rabbis. There are thirty-five large congregations of more than a thousand families that have assistant rabbis on their staff and every two and three years energetically look to replace these assistant rabbis who move on to their own pulpits.

To further exacerbate the problem, in the combined Cincinnati–New York class of forty-eight fledgling rabbis that graduated in 2000—the seventeen from Cincinnati constituted one of the smallest classes to be ordained there in many years—over half of the graduates were not interested in seeking congregational pulpits. With their rabbinical degrees, these ordinees were interested in pursuing strictly noncongregational opportunities in academe, in American Jewish organizational life, and in the military and community-counseling chaplaincies. This "nonpulpit rabbinate" is an unpublicized but highly dramatic sea change which has taken place in our movement and bears directly upon the present shortage of pulpit rabbis. In the year of my ordination, 1951, I cannot remember a single ordinee contemplating turning down the pulpit rabbinate for a nonpulpit career. Students traditionally entered rabbinical school in my generation, and in the generations before, with the commanding and exclusive career goal of serving the congregational Reform rabbinate in every one of its multifaceted spiritual, liturgical, scholarly, educational, pastoral, administrative, and ambassadorial Jewish roles.

As the years passed in my own rabbinical career, there were, here and there, a few instances where a fellow classmate left the rabbinate voluntarily to pursue a more personally fulfilling career in a totally different field. There were also a number of colleagues who were driven out of their congregations as a result of scandalous rabbinical behavior, either personal or professional. More frequently, however, leaving the pulpit rabbinate was a shameful and bitter case of some colleague becoming an innocent, career-destroyed victim of ugly and nefarious lay-rabbinical political power games.

Some of my colleagues who eventually chose to opt out of pulpits either voluntarily or by lay collusion should, in truth, probably never have entered rabbinical school in the first place. The rabbinate and public life in general were probably never a wise or realistic choice for them. Our seminary, too, bears a significant part of the blame and responsibility for many of these turbulent and broken rabbinical careers. The professional screening process for students seeking admission to enroll in HUC-JIR when I began my graduate school studies in 1947 was a joke.

Substantive professional profiling of the candidate's psychological and emotional suitability for Jewish public life was nonexistent when I was interviewed a half-century ago. The average candidate needed only a bachelor of arts degree, a minimum proficiency with the Hebrew language, some evidence of having grown up Jewishly, a handful of character references, and a strong verbal commitment before the interviewing committee evidencing that he sincerely wanted to study for the rabbinate and serve the Jewish community and Reform Judaism as a liberal rabbi.

By the end of our freshman year at rabbinical school, if not sooner, particularly in a small class of thirteen students like mine, it was not too difficult to form a gut judgment as to who really didn't belong there and who seemed to be headed for a troubled future after ordination. The real scandal of this whole interviewing procedure is that a half-century since my postwar generation applied for admission, the psychological screening process in New York and Cincinnati, from what my young assistants have confided to me, is still so woefully superficial and nonintensive as to ensure the acceptance of all but the most flamingly sociopathic applicant.

Our student body at the New York school in the immediate post–World War II years was a highly unprecedented mixture of graduate students. Many of us were returning veterans who had just come back from military service to complete our war-interrupted university degrees. I, for example, had left the City College of New York at the end of my sophomore year and at the tender age of eighteen, with two years of college behind me, had enlisted in the Army Signal Corps in the winter of 1942. I served overseas as a noncommissioned cryptographic officer for two years in New Guinea and the Philippines, and ended up among the first occupation troops in Japan in the fall of 1945. Upon being discharged, I returned to CCNY and received my bachelor's degree in June of 1947. That summer I applied for admission to rabbinical school and began my formal rabbinical studies in the fall of 1947.

What made my rabbinical class in New York unique was this heady and volatile mix of war veterans from all walks of Jewish life. A large number of the students in our entering class were graduates of yeshiva-type Orthodox Jewish educations. While these students were personally very traditional in their family and academic backgrounds, they were at the same time conscious escapees from the rigors and confines of having grown up in Orthodoxy. I was probably the only member of my entire class in New York who was actually a second -generation Reform Jew, not to mention the son of a Reform rabbi and the nephew of a Reform rabbi— ordained, respectively, in 1915 and 1916 at the Hebrew Union College in Cincinnati, then the bastion of classical Reform Judaism. My cousin Daniel Silver, of blessed memory, and I were the sixth generation of rabbis in the Silver rabbinic line, from our paternal grandfather, Rabbi Moses Silver, and the three generations before him who had all been Orthodox rabbis in Lithuania.

What was amazing, if not shocking, about my grandfather was that he actively encouraged both of his sons, my father, Maxwell, and my uncle, Abba Hillel, to become *Reform* rabbis! His was the fervent and far-seeing conviction, as far back as the first decade of the twentieth century, that the exploding and developing American Jewish community of the future was headed in the direction of a non-Orthodox type of liberal Judaism. He boldly envisioned a future American Jewish community that would hopefully be deeply grounded in the intellectual and ritual best of the Jewish past and yet with no fear of modernizing Judaism so that it could flower and grow stronger in this promising but radically different American Jewish milieu.

My grandfather, Rabbi Moses Silver, was also quite unique in his Orthodox generation of traditional rabbis for another compelling reason. He was one of the few Orthodox rabbis of that turn-of-the-century time who was a proud and passionate Zionist. He was keenly anxious for both of his sons to push the Zionist cause strenuously at rabbinical school in Cincinnati in what was then considered to be the hotbed of classical German Reform anti-Zionism. A generation later, during the 1930s, Abba Hillel Silver was almost single-handedly responsible for influencing the majority of American Reform rabbis to repudiate the historic anti-Zionism of the late nineteenth and early twentieth centuries. Abba Hillel Silver also militantly led his Reform colleagues to create the climate in the postwar era for the entire Reform Jewish movement, lay and rabbinic, to actively and proudly support the cause of Jewish nationalism in Palestine.

Several decades after I was ordained in 1951, all entering candidates for the Reform rabbinate were mandated to spend the first year of the five- year graduate school rabbinical program at the Jerusalem branch of our seminary. It was fervently hoped that the future leaders of the American Reform rabbinate would not only hone their Hebrew-speaking skills in the State of Israel, but that the experience there of successive generations of Reform rabbis would inspire the entire Reform Jewish movement in America to relate warmly and actively in behalf of the reborn Jewish state, where the ultimate destinies of the two greatest communities in all of Jewish history were to be forever bound up together.

It is my strong belief that the growing shortage of pulpit rabbis has not been confronted realistically by our seminary or by our congregational lay leaders. In my mind, the number-one shameful reality is that the bulk of American Jewish youth are not being sufficiently educated in their Judaism to warrant their seriously considering a career in the rabbinate. The leading culprit here is the scandalous post–Bar and Bat Mitzvah dropout rate among thirteen-year-old Jewish boys and girls. Using my own Congregation Beth Israel (averaging fourteen hundred families) as a common gauge during the 1950s through the 1970s, the majority of our thirteen-year-old youngsters at that time routinely remained in religious school after Bar/Bat Mitzvah for at least three additional years of continuing early-teenage Jewish education. At the end of the tenth grade, they were then routinely confirmed en masse upon their sixteenth birthday. A small but goodly number of post-confirmands elected to continue their Jewish education in an eleventh- and twelfth-grade congregational program of pre-college Jewish studies.

However, in the late 1970s and up to the time I retired in 1993 after forty-three years in the rabbinate, the Bar/Bat Mitzvah dropout rate in the congregation dramatically rose to almost 50 percent, and it has sadly done the same throughout our entire movement in congregations large and small. With the arrival of the twenty-first century, the dropout figures promise to climb even higher; new generations of young Jews after the age of thirteen will undoubtedly continue to disappear into a black hole of mounting teenage and collegiate Jewish ignorance, illiteracy, indifference, and detachment from the Jewish community. When one is chillingly confronted with the utterly minimalist system of Jewish education today and in the future—a Jewish education pitiably arrested at the immature age of thirteen—it should not really be that difficult or that surprising for American Jewish rabbinical and lay leaders to see why the best and brightest of our career-contemplating college-age Jewish student population rarely consider choosing the rabbinate of all professions as an attractive, desirable, and fulfilling lifetime career. On the plus side, however, a large number of our Jewish youth have been and still are attracted to many other honorable lifetime careers where, as in the rabbinate, the opportunities for human and spiritual outreach and societal repair are equally calling and rewarding.

In his crisply written but essentially despairing new book, *The Will to Live On*, Herman Wouk projects a truly bleak future for the American Jewish community. Notwithstanding his own late-adult personal discovery of a fierce attachment to Orthodox Judaism, which he wrote about rhapsodically a generation ago in *This Is My God*, Wouk is still the first to admit that American Orthodoxy, comprising today less than 10 percent of American Jews, is no wave of the religious future in the United States. Of America's six million Jews, half of that total are affiliated with Reform, Conservative, and Reconstructionist Judaism. The remaining 40 percent have no formal affiliation with any movement.

Looking ahead to the next half-century, one does not have to be a Herman Wouk to predict that few of the presently unaffiliated will be drawn into the three major non-Orthodox movements and even fewer will be attracted to Orthodoxy. The alarmingly high and still growing rate of intermarriage and assimilation in this country will also probably continue to diminish the high numbers of unaffiliated Jews. Wouk dismisses both affiliated and unaffiliated non-Orthodox Jews as "running on empty." That is to say, American Jews, by and large, have so watered down and trivialized the historical

Jewish faith, he bitterly charges, that there is little of authentic Jewish substance left— theologically, intellectually, culturally, and ritually—to guarantee an American Jewish future worthy of the name.

Despite the stepped-up intensity of Wouk's most recent screed against non-Orthodoxy, those of us in the nontraditional Jewish majority in this country would have to fully agree with him that cutting Jewish education dead in its tracks at the age of pubescence will only guarantee a Jewishly-empty future generation. More to the point, it will be a generation ill-equipped intellectually and religiously, woefully uninterested in providing a rabbinic leadership worthy of the name, not to mention sustaining a committed and quality lay leadership.

What they do not teach us at rabbinical school, whether in my day or even half a century later, is that neither we nor the congregations that employ us can possibly fulfill the job description of the modern-day rabbinate. No matter how gifted our background, no matter how deeply and personally committed we are to serving God and our people, the rabbinic roles we are routinely, collectively, and single-handedly expected to perform upon ordination and throughout our lifetime career in the average congregation basically defy do-ability and sanity. The day has not yet arrived, and probably never will, when one man or woman will combine within his or her rabbinical skills the vast complex of lay-expected multi-demands of charismatic preacher, scholarly teacher, compassionate pastor, savvy ecumenical ambassador, artful corporate-type CEO administrator, professional educator, guitar-wielding spiritual pied-piper to the young, miracle-working counselor for marriages on the rocks, and, toughest of all, traditional defender of the faith for so many of little faith.

The word is clearly out to Jewish career weighers and watchers, young and old, that the rabbinate as it has existed for over two millennia has become a thing of rich history—but history nonetheless for the Reform, Conservative, and

Reconstructionist congregations that comprise over 90 percent of the affiliated American Jewish community. That our seminary leadership and national lay Jewish leaders remain completely blind to the compelling need for a radical reconfiguration of the modern-day rabbinate is no mystery for us rabbis in the field. This is not to ignore a handful of my gifted colleagues who have uncommonly managed to balance the balls of rabbinic complexity and responsibility with consummate éclat, mastery, and fulfillment. But I can assure you that this tiny percentage of spiritual exemplars in our profession is in no way representative of the majority of my colleagues, who, whether they expected it or not, are locked tight into careers of gnawing frustration and minimal fulfillment.

Our rabbinical schools do a first-class job in seeing to it that the average ordinee, after five intensive years of scholarly study, achieves a solid mastery of classic, medieval, and contemporary Jewish knowledge and is fully prepared to assume the historic role of the rabbi as teacher which is what the title "rabbi" has primarily meant in Jewish history. The problem, however, with the academic faculties at rabbinical schools past and present is that most of them have no first- hand personal experience as congregational rabbis in the field. Most of the faculty are first and foremost impressive scholars. But they are woefully ill-equipped to prepare their students to cope with the vastly different worlds of the old-time East European shtetl milieu of the traditional rabbi (the "Rav") and the modern- day impossible world of the typical non-Orthodox spiritual leader serving the average American Jewish community.

That is to say, from Minsk to Memphis, from Kovno to Kansas City, from Helm to Cincinnati, we are dealing here with radically different, totally dissimilar, and irrecoverable Jewish worlds. From a basically one-dimensional tight Orthodox Jewish society of old where the rabbi ruled supreme by virtue of knowledge, lineage, and legal mandate, today's multidenominational, non-Orthodox American Jewish world finds the rabbi no longer at the epicenter of community power and influence. It is no longer a secret that the modern-day non-Orthodox rabbi has been relegated to the outer periphery of Jewish communal life and influence. The new wrinkle is the dramatic emergence of oftentimes Jewishly incompetent lay power and influence in the Jewish community which has not only marginalized rabbinic decision-making but in all too many cases has tyrannized over our profession.

This has had a growingly frustrating, if not chilling, impact upon a great number of my colleagues, young and old, who are not only becoming seriously disenchanted serving the Jewish people but are consciously and unconsciously communicating their professional unease, disillusionment, and unhappiness to legions of young men and women, in or out of the congregation, who may be giving some serious thought to a rabbinic career. Whenever the best and brightest of the young have turned to me over the years for my own personal and frank critique of the modern-day rabbinate, I have never failed to be brutally honest about the pitfalls as well as the fulfillments of this profession. Perhaps the biggest pitfall I have shared with them is to compel the career-seeker to confront what I consider to be the quandary of quandaries in considering the rabbinate as one's profession: That is to say, is this particular young person emotionally, psychologically, and spiritually cut out for the utterly bizarre demands and never-ending complex pressures of public life in general and Jewish public life in particular? Truth be told, many of those coming into the field, and far more practicing in the field, all too quickly realize that they are not, and never really were in any meaningful way, emotionally and psychologically built for the rabbinate. Few of us in the field, in fact, have been able to micromanage the awesome burden of struggling to live a satisfying public and personal life never completely on our own. Few of us can be expected to raise a family where spouse and children must be shared disproportionately with congregational and communal calendar needs and demands. Few of even my most accomplished colleagues are successful in rabbinically ricocheting, back and forth, with revolving short terms of presidential and board lay leadership where levels of synagogue captaincy and serious Jewish commitment often range from rare exemplary to mind-blowing ineptitude. Rarely do enough of our colleagues find ultimate career satisfaction and fulfillment in grappling with a mass membership, whether in a large or small congregation, whom they may or may not significantly affect but twice a year on Rosh Hashanah and Yom Kippur.

This is only the short list of anomalies, incongruities, and "catch 22" circumstances that unduly dog my profession and seriously deter recruitment efforts to expand the dwindling pool of student seminarians. Until these darker and deeply complex sides of both the modern-day non-Orthodox congregation and the contemporary pulpit rabbinate are honestly and realistically confronted and boldly reconfigured by the best and brightest of our combined rabbinical and lay leadership in this country, the rapidly dwindling rabbinic supply will never meet the full rabbinic demand. Whether career and personal expectations can possibly be creatively (and satisfactorily) reconfigured in this country is highly uncertain. The twain, in truth, may never ever really mesh. But to fill both pulpit and pew, it still behooves us to make a herculean effort to try to understand the basic dilemma and find out what desperately needs to be done.

3

What Do You Find Most Wonderful About Each Other? What Do You Find Most Obnoxious About Each Other?
(or, The Fine Art of Premarital Counseling)

Lay people call rabbis for all sorts of appointments dealing with some upcoming life- cycle event in their lives—the birth of a child, a Bar or Bat Mitzvah, a wedding, a potential conversion, a death in the family. They generally expect that the rabbinic encounters will yield helpful and vital information and guidance which will enable them to cope more effectively with the stresses and challenges surrounding the event that concerns them. When the life-cycle event is a premarital conference, I have always, throughout my rabbinical career, deliberately set the young couple up for a totally unexpected and sometimes nerve-wracking counseling session. If more of my colleagues were to adopt my somewhat unorthodox approach, premarital couples, young or old, would come away from such encounters with a far more honest and realistic conviction as to whether their pending marriage was truly made in heaven or possibly scripted for hell.

The first jolt the adoring couple experiences after the pleasantries are exchanged is that they learn from me that the prime purpose of our meeting in advance of their marriage really has little to do with "getting" married. In most cases, they come in expecting the totality of the premarital conference to focus strictly upon coordinating the many logistics of the ceremony. These include the signing of the civil and religious documents, allowable witnesses, the traditional marching order of the bridal party, what type of music is acceptable in the sanctuary, where parents and divorced parents are to be safely positioned, whether or not to gamble on the perilous risk of toddler ring-bearers and petal strewers, aesthetically pairing ushers and bridesmaids by height, heft, and hair, prepping the bride and groom to vocalize their wedding vows to each other in unslaughterable Hebrew, how to deal with jammed ring fingers and glasses that resist repeated foot smashing, and how to cope generally with "under the chuppah" emotions ranging all the way from catatonic nervousness to mood-shattering tears, giggles, and wisecracks.

All of the above I have routinely managed to sort out over the years in relatively short order, paving the way for what I consider to be the real meat of the meeting. Unfortunately, too many rabbis and clergy fail to deal with crucial and substantive matters in these premarital interviews. Even in the early years of my rabbinate, before the general and Jewish divorce rate went through the roof, I intuitively felt that the logistics of "getting married" were crowding out the vital opportunity to focus in on the techniques of what it essentially takes for the average couple to stay married. To get the couple to really open up with me and with each other—as to what initially drew them together, what they saw in each other, what they wanted and needed from each other, what was perhaps missing in their relationship, and how they were planning to deal with that in the future—I routinely made it my prime counseling technique to throw them each the same provocative initial question. "Of all of your fiancée's most *wonderful* qualities," I would initially ask, "which grabs you the most?" What then usually poured forth freely and adoringly from both of their lips and hearts were touching paeans of mutual praise highlighting each other's innate goodness, kindness, tenderness, compassion, humor, stability, maturing, caring, giving, and sharing. With all of these ecstatic "positives" going for them, how this seemed always to augur splendidly for their future married life together!

Then I would drop my premarital bombshell: "Tell me, now, both of you, what can't you stand about each other? No one, after all, is perfect. If you could change just *one* thing about your lover, what would it be?" Then the mutual squirming would begin in earnest. A long and embarrassed silence generally hung in the air, each blubberingly offering the other the privilege of confessing first. With my gentle prodding, the faucet of their inner feelings would slowly open wide and then a torrent of darker, negative character traits began to spew forth. At times, what came from their lips rocked us all in our seats. "I can't stand your stubbornness; you're an unforgiving bitch; you treat my mother like shit; you're afraid of taking a chance; you really don't respect my opinions; you're a goddamn slob; you have no taste in clothing; I can't stand how you eat; you don't know how to relax; you're only tender with me when you want sex; you make me feel like a complete moron because I never finished college; you're always looking at the dark and despairing side of life . . ."

These are but a bare handful of the explosive snippets of negative, biting dialogue that I have managed over the years to elicit from premarital couples sitting before me. I must confess that it wasn't really that shocking to hear these bitter and recriminatory outbursts because early on in my career I quickly sensed that below the surface of every couple's loving relationship there were always a host of unspoken and repressed areas of dissatisfaction, frustration, and unhappiness. Every couple in a marriage or on the threshold of marriage is intuitively aware of mutual inner shortcomings and imperfections.

My urging each couple to bring up these highly sensitive "neg-atives" during the premarital conference, while admittedly opening up a can of worms, has always proven always to be enormously helpful in compelling the average couple, *before* they got married, to be brutally honest and open with each other.

What always stunned me, however, in premarital counsel-ing throughout the length and breadth of my rabbinical career, was to see not only what young couples *withheld* from each other, even in the longest courtships, but what they never ever really truly knew about each other! One of the hairiest out-bursts in this connection—I remember it to this day, and it occurred in my study over two decades ago—was when a young man was excitedly sharing with me his future plans and dreams revolving around his passionately wanting to have at least three or four children. His fiancée listened quietly and somewhat grimly to his ranting on about the joys of parent-hood. With teeth clenched tightly and jaw fixed sternly, she waited as long as she could and then she proceeded to lash out at him, almost venomously, "I don't *ever* want to have a child!" This was virtually spat into his face. The potential groom just sat there for a moment completely stunned, as I was. And then, coming out of his shock, he turned bitterly to her and wailed: "You never told me that! In the three years we've been going together and talking about getting married, you never once mentioned a single word to me about not wanting to have a family! You've always known how nuts I am about having kids. Why didn't you bring this up ages ago?"

I was ready to crawl under my desk. I squirmed not so much because this couple was hotly engaged in an ugly shout-ing match in my study, which in many a counseling session is de rigueur. I was mainly depressed because this young woman had obviously never had the guts to level openly with her fiancé about her deep, inner feelings as to never ever wanting to have any children. I held no brief against her about her very own personal convictions regarding motherhood. That was strictly her privilege. Loads of couples I have counseled over the years, for good reasons of their own which I fully respected, preferred childless marriages. That's their own free and mutually agreed upon choice. But this young woman in my study had been so grossly stupid as to keep this secret from her fiancé until this very moment in my study on the very threshold of their marriage.

After I got them both to cool down, I advised them to put their wedding plans on hold. I urged them to seek out some professional counseling surrounding this very delicate and divisive matter that would help them to determine whether their marriage was still viable in the light of their passionate differences of opinion about having children. Several months later, the groom called to tell me that after extensive counseling, they had decided together not to get married. I wished the young man well, and I hoped that one day soon he would find a woman who shared his strong feelings about parenthood and family.

That premarital conference emboldened me with every successive meeting to ferret out, as sensitively or as bluntly as I could, the areas of gut incompatibility which I sensed that the average couple, deep-down, was simply afraid to talk about or come to grips with and resolve *before* marriage. Most couples believe that as the years go by their passionate love for each other will enable them to cope with their differences at least to the point where they do not seriously damage or totally destroy the marriage. With all deference to the heat and intensity of the genuine love that the average couple professed for each other in my premarital counseling, I always made it my prime rabbinical business to warn them that far more than romantic love is essential to guarantee a lifetime of marital happiness and fulfillment.

Over the years, I challenged each couple to hone at least two specific marital skills as surefire preventatives for marriage breakdown. Skill number one was *communication,* the free-flowing ability to verbalize to each other at all times their deepest and most private feelings touching upon almost everything near and dear in their relationship. I would routinely ask each partner: "On a scale of one to ten, how do you frankly rate each other's ability and capacity to speak the truth about things that truly annoy and anguish you in your relationship?" Rare was the occasion in my counseling where both partners gave each other a perfect ten. In more cases than not, they freely admitted that they had a considerable way to go to match their communication skills. Mature love, I attempted to warn each couple, was *total* openness and oftentimes a raw but loving candor and gut honesty that many couples frankly were not prepared to handle. But if they were prepared to let it all hang out, they could work their way harmoniously through each and every marital crisis and immeasurably strengthen and enhance their marriage in the process.

Another counseling seed I always planted in their minds was to be prepared to seek out a *third* party, professional or respected nonprofessional, who could help them break any communication freeze that might threaten to sour if not destroy their relationship. I reminded them how grateful we should all be to live in a generation where resorting to professional marital counseling was looked upon as a potential blessing and salvation and no longer as a family or personal scandal or shame. Obviously, there are no guarantees that professional counseling will automatically resolve every conceivable marital problem. But without it, the pattern in far too many cases was to leap-frog bitterly to the lawyers and the divorce courts. Jews can be particularly grateful that if a marriage is basically and irreparably doomed, there is no shame or sin attached to getting divorced. Throughout history, Jewish law has always realistically provided for divorce when all reasonable hope for the future of the marriage was irretrievably shattered. The tragedy of so many divorces in our generation, however, is that vast numbers of them could have been salvaged if, very early on in the relationship, far more attention had been paid by each partner to improving basic communication skills.

Beyond the compelling, ongoing need to verbalize their innermost thoughts to each other, the final challenge I always left with the premarital couples was to ask each of them this last question: "In the vocabulary of love, which word, above all, is indispensable for *any* marriage to succeed?" What generally leapt to their lips were words like "sensitivity," "compassion," "humor," "compromise," "optimism," "sexuality," and "mutual respect." Without question, I agreed, *all* of these were basic ingredients utterly essential for any successful and truly fulfilling marriage. There was, however, one other absolutely high-priority word that was rarely mentioned by either partner. That word is the simple four-letter word "work."

My last caveat to the couple was that if they truly wanted their marriage to succeed, it was not going to happen automatically. Every single day of their future relationship, they must come to understand, was going to entail pure, hard, loving work, energy, effort, and sacrifice. In order to persist and deepen and grow even more wondrous as the years go by love demands total, ongoing concentration upon each other's daily, never-ending needs, wants, demands, eccentricities, and differences. If the couple were solemnly committed to "work" at their love in this mutually aggressive spirit—never for a single moment taking each other for granted—then each successive milestone anniversary in their marriage would inevitably see the marriage reach indescribably higher and deeper levels of marital happiness and fulfillment.

I generally wrapped up my premarital conferences with the parting challenge: "You think that you love each other *now* as deeply as two people could ever love one another! I do not contest that for a single moment. But what you elect to *do* for each other in the immediate future; what you will choose to *give* to each other; what you will ultimately *demand* of each other; what you will eventually decide to *sacrifice* for each other; what you, over a lifetime, will fully *invest* in each other—only the years ahead will determine whether this kind of mutual lifetime 'work' will blessedly succeed."

4

Your Visit Means the World to Me, Rabbi!

(or, Pastoral Calling: Its Hazards and Its Rewards)

Five chilling pastoral visits during my forty-three years in the rabbinate have remained to haunt me to this day. I'm grateful that they all took place at the very beginning of my career. They steeled me immeasurably for what was to come.

My first traumatic pastoral call took place in a mental ward lock-up. A member of my congregation had called me on the phone and beseeched me to visit her emotionally ill twenty-four-year-old son who had been institutionalized there for many months. This was in that distant era when many patients were incarcerated in psychiatric facilities for interminable periods of time. This particular hospital actually enjoyed a national reputation, and some very famous celebrities from many different fields went to "dry out" periodically from alcohol and drug abuse. There were also troubled lives in almost permanent residence there with little or no chance for recovery. Today, of course, the entire psychiatric-hospital scene is radically different. Strict and complex new legal guidelines from within and without the medical profession and managed health care organizations sharply limit medical stays in all hospitals and institutions—even for the most severe cases.

When I finally paid my pastoral call upon this young man, the old mental health system still prevailed. Right up front, I must confess that dealing with cases of severe emotional illness, in or out of hospital settings, generally freaked me out. If I felt, as a rabbi, ill at ease because of my rabbinical school's lack of professional training in the areas of marriage and divorce counseling, as alluded to in another chapter, I felt positively helpless and almost fearful when confronting parishioners in mental extremis. My personal knowledge of mental illness was narrowly limited to a teenage fascination with the human brain, when I had done some serious reading in the writings of the world-famous psychiatrist Dr. Karl Menninger. Digging into his classic and pioneering 1930 work, *The Human Mind*, I toyed for quite some time with the idea of becoming a psychiatrist. About the closest rabbinical students of my generation came into contact with serious studies in the field of psychology and mental illness was our in-depth classroom contact with Moses Maimonides's twelfth-century *Guide for the Perplexed*, which was, however, very short on science and medicine but long and mind-challenging in the field of medieval philosophy and logic.

My only other significant personal contact with emotional disorder was the cyclical, post-partem depression which my mother periodically suffered with for years after my birth. For many harrowing weeks each year, like clockwork, she went regularly into a deep emotional depression that totally incapacitated her. As mysteriously and as regularly as she went into these annual depressions at home, nothing was ever able to shorten her emotional *Sturm und Drang* to the great frustration of a network of doctors and specialists who tried almost everything to relieve her condition—shock treatment, psychotherapy, drugs, you name it. Depression plagued her throughout her adult life. The miracle was that when her depression mysteriously lifted, she carried on her marital, family, and social life with great relish and satisfaction. As I say, her illness gave me my first-hand utterly helpless exposure to this grievous type of mental disorder, which probably was singly responsible for making me hypersensitive, hyperhelpless, and hyperfearful in confronting emotional disorders in and beyond the family.

In any event, when I finally visited the mental hospital to pay my call upon this young man at the behest of his mother, I approached his private room with great trepidation. The nurse's aide unlocked the door to his room and shouted in: "Marvin—you've got a visitor! Your rabbi has come to see you." Marvin was prone on his bed, and it appeared that he was napping when we bolted in. The aide let me in and told me that when I was through with visiting Marvin, just bang on the door and he would let me out. He quickly closed the door shut behind me! I almost plotzed when I heard the aide locking Marvin and me in the room.

Marvin slowly rose to his feet and sullenly stared at me with a somewhat surly and forbidding sneer. "Who the hell are *you*? he finally said. "I'm your rabbi, Marvin. Your mother asked me to visit you. How are you feeling today? I'm sorry to have disturbed your nap. How are they treating you here?"

Marvin didn't answer for what seemed like an eternity, which made me even more nervous. He just kept glowering at me darkly. I was about to pound on the door and yell for the aide to let me out — or at least to leave the door open. After what seemed like ages, Marvin yelled at me, "You're not a rabbi!"

Trying to maintain my composure, I assured Marvin of my rabbinic credentials, but he would have none of it. I even reached into my wallet and nervously pulled out my driver's license, which had my name and clergy title in bold print on it, and I flashed it in Marvin's face. He grabbed it out of my hands and studied it intently and silently. Finally, he looked me squarely in the eye, shook his head angrily, and bounded over to the door—rapping on it loudly. The aide came quickly and unlocked the door. Marvin yelled at him, "Get this bastard out of here! He's passing himself off as some sort of rabbi. I don't want to have anything to do with him. Get him out!"

The aide sheepishly and apologetically looked at me and shrugged his head. I bolted from the room. I told the aide not to worry. Obviously, Marvin was not in the mood to see rabbis today. As I fled down the corridor, in a fit of panic and relief, I shouted back to Marvin that I'd pop by another day and would give his mother his love.

A second, totally different kind of mental hospital visit has also remained in my embarrassed memory for years. A husband from my former congregation in Pittsburgh called me one day to ask me to visit his wife. Her doctor had very recently admitted her to a psychiatric ward for intensive evaluation.

This pastoral visit also came at the very beginning of my rabbinate. The young woman was about my age. She seemed delighted that I had come to visit her. We conversed freely and warmly in her private room, and she charmed me with her intelligence and gracious composure. All the while, as we sat talking, I was wondering to myself what in God's name she was doing in a mental lock-up.

After we had chatted easily together for some time, she suddenly stopped talking and broke down into sobbing. She begged me to speak to the psychiatrist in charge of her case and demand that she be released from the hospital and allowed to go home to her husband. She wailed, "Rabbi, I don't belong here! You, as a rabbi, can get me out." To stop her from crying, which had really unglued me, I promised that when I left her room I would try to find her doctor and see if she could be released.

The doctor was not in, but I quickly found the head nurse and pompously demanded, as the patient's rabbi, that she get in touch with the doctor and tell him that in my "professional" judgment, this woman really didn't belong in the lock-up and would thrive immeasurably better at home.

Before the day was out, the woman was released and sent home on the heels of my intervention. Within another forty-eight hours, her husband and doctor brought her back to the hospital, where she truly belonged, notwithstanding my rabbinical naiveté and totally juvenile comprehension of psychiatric illness and procedures. For years afterwards, in the midst of my hospital calling, I never allowed myself to intervene in complex medical situations, sensing that I was way over my pastoral head.

The third pastoral nightmare, which also chills me to this very day, was my visit, early on in my career, to an elderly, critically ill patient-member at the behest of his wife. When I got to this man's room, I knocked gently on his door and peeked in to let him know that I was there. He appeared to be resting comfortably. I noticed that his eyes were open and seemingly staring at the ceiling.

I sat down quietly in the chair next to his bed, introduced myself, and told him that if he wished I could come back at another more convenient time. He did not respond in any visible way, and yet his open eyes remained riveted to the ceiling. I figured that he was just not in the mood to talk. I pressed on somewhat uneasily and told him that his wife was very anxious about him, sent him her most fervent prayers, and would be in to see him sometime later.

As I continued trying to engage him in conversation, a nurse came into the room. With the grimmest of looks, she asked me, "And who are *you*?" I introduced myself to her as the patient's rabbi. She gasped. "Oh, Reverend, didn't they tell you at the nurses' desk? Mr. Schwartz is dead! He expired about twenty minutes ago. Pathology is on the way up to move his body to the hospital morgue. I'm so sorry you were not alerted! When I left him a short time ago, I should have closed his eyes. Forgive me, Reverend! Did you want to say a prayer or something before we get him out of here?"

Half-numb with shock, I mumbled a fast and shaken "Shema Yisroel" and fled. In all of my subsequent hospital visitations, I have never failed to stop first at the nurse's station to find out whether the patient was "in" or somewhat more "up" for my ministrations!

My fourth jolting pastoral call at the local hospital centered around another young husband, who told me that his wife was recovering nicely from a hysterectomy and would really welcome a visit from me. Several days passed, and I made my way to the hospital to pay her a call. It was late in the afternoon and rather quiet in the corridor outside her room. Her door was closed, but I could hear what clearly sounded like laughter and giggling inside. I tapped gently on the door, but no one inside responded. And yet, the laughing continued. Undaunted, I rapped on the door again, opened it ever so slightly, and diffidently stuck my head into the room.

Lo and behold, the husband and wife were buck naked in bed and going at it sexually—completely oblivious to my utterly shocked rabbinical presence. I shut their door immediately. To this very day, I don't believe that they were ever aware of my dutiful and eye-popping pastoral intrusion. Every time I bumped into both of them at the temple, I simply smiled weakly and blushed silently.

The fifth and final emotionally jarring pastoral visitation, which also remains with me after nearly five decades of nightmare-recall, was the night, ages ago, when the phone rang next to my bed long after midnight. Aroused uneasily from a deep slumber, I picked up the phone and listened somewhat blearily to the frantic caller—another member of my congregation—who begged me to come immediately to the local hospital, where his wife was in labor and screaming for her rabbi.

I really did not know this couple well at all. I vaguely remembered that the wife was a nurse, and that this was their first child. I told the frantic husband that I would get out of bed immediately and pop right over. I told him to meet me outside of the delivery room, where he could fill me in with more details. I sped immediately to the hospital. It was about two in the morning, and the young, heavy-breathing husband met me outside the delivery room in a state of near panic. He said that her obstetrician had come out of the delivery room about a half-hour ago and told him that there were some medical complications but that the situation was not life-threatening. The doctor had also explained that because his wife was a delivery room nurse who was au courant with difficult delivery procedures, she probably had a premonition that something was drastically wrong and that they weren't telling her the complete story. She had become quite hysterical and was calling out for her rabbi. I asked the husband whether his wife had called for *him* to go inside the delivery room, where he could perhaps better help to calm her. He said that he was scared shitless to go inside. "Rabbi," he pleaded, "I'd only faint dead away in there. I can't stand the sight of blood!" "Marvin," I confessed to him (God forbid, yet another Marvin in my young ministry), "*I'm* even *more* squeamish about blood than you are! I want you to know that I've never ever been inside a delivery room in my own personal or professional life. If I have to go in there to meet with your wife, I'll probably faint dead away myself!" "Rabbi" he pleaded, "husband or no husband, I can't go inside. And, anyway, she's yelling for *you* and not for me!"

At that point, the obstetrician, whom I knew casually, came out, spotted me talking with the husband, grabbed my hand, and whisked me into the delivery room. Marvin's wife was spread–eagled nude on the delivery table, while several doctors and nurses were struggling to bring her baby out of her bloody womb. The wife, on seeing me, put a visor-like lock on my two hands and wailed inconsolably that she was going to die!

I looked at the doctor beseechingly for some professional confirmation about her plight. Both he and the nurse beside him shook their heads vigorously, indicating that she was *not* dying, and that everything would be all right. While they kept working on her at their end of the operating table, I kept assuring her on my end that she was just fine. As calmly as I could, with my eyes shut tight, and my knees starting to buckle, I kept up the litany, "Just calm down, Sarah. Get a grip on yourself. In *no* way are you in danger."

In about twenty minutes, the baby came out. Little by little, Sarah's crying and terror subsided, and mother and son were just fine. Sarah still never let up on iota on her fierce grip of my hands. It was probably just as well, because it prevented me from either passing out or bolting bodily from the room, which is all I wanted to do during the entire time I was entrapped. Long after this pastoral trauma had concluded, I was at least somewhat thankful that my own deep revulsion at the sight of blood had entered into a less fearsome and heart-stopping mode both in my professional and my personal life. I could handle *any* pastoral crisis now!

While these five emotionally draining incidents early on in my rabbinate shook me up intensely, and made me question my pastoral effectiveness, as the years went by I managed to gain invaluable experience and deep fulfillment in hospital and home pastoral calling. I still, however, never lost my anger at my rabbinical school for catapulting me and my classmates into this momentous phase of our profession with such a pitifully limited background in human and pastoral relations. I am pleased to see that it is a shade better for the present generation of young rabbis—but not that much.

Three specific kinds of hospital calling never failed to be of positive value. In the lowest-priority category there is the pastoral drop-in visit to the patient who is hospitalized for a non-life-threatening illness or medical procedure. In this situation, the rabbi's visit is generally unexpected by the patient and sometimes even undesired. Frankly, many of these members were quite surprised, if not totally shocked, to see their rabbi at their bedside. The typical reaction was usually: "Who told you that I was sick?" Invariably, I replied, "A little birdie told me."

Most members were generally unaware that the clergy, in their regular weekly rounds, first check the lists prepared by the hospital for clergy of all faiths to discover who of their members are there, whether they want to be visited or not. Hospitals for years have routinely asked admitting patients or families for their congregational and religious affiliation. Those who specifically wanted no visitation simply answered that they had no congregational tie. Little did they realize, however, that their names were then automatically put into the noncongregational alphabetized list of admitted patients. The savvy clergyman would then simply check both affiliated and nonaffiliated lists against his own congregational roster to make sure that no one was missed.

If you came up with a "live one" from your congregation, you would then simply pop up to the room and pay your respects. In this basically low-priority visitation category, what I discovered early on in my career was that just dropping by, even briefly, was enormously appreciated. It gave many of us clergy a very meaningful entrée into a member's life, an opportunity that in a very large congregation like mine could be frustratingly missed. The bottom line for this kind of member reaction was generally, "I really appreciate that you cared enough to come by even if I didn't need you and never wanted you to come."

A significantly higher priority of hospital call was a visit to a member who was hospitalized for more critical reasons. Up to the last decade of my career, patients recovering from various surgeries enjoyed the luxury of extended hospitalization. Today, outrageously, if you're allowed a stay exceeding forty-eight hours—even after major surgery—you're probably near death. Short stay or long, however, when the rabbi comes calling, I've discovered over the years that many patients are quite anxious to unburden themselves, even if their relationship with the clerical visitor was superficial or even nonexistent before the illness.

I discovered early on in my career that there is an exquisitely delicate moment in such seemingly routine visits where the timing is mystically ripe for the frankest and most meaningful dialogue dealing with all sorts of marital, family, or career issues. What generally precipitates this threshold moment in hospital calling is the patient's scary confrontation with death and the resulting urge to connect at this key moment with a potentially helpful, eager, and comforting professional.

I cannot begin to count the vast number of members who over the years, in the three congregations I served, for whom the hospital bedside setting turned out to be a rare moment of ultimate member-rabbi emotional and spiritual breakthrough. However, I must also be honest enough to confess that too many were the sad times, long after these tender hospital "melt-down" visits occurred, when the same once-hospitalized members, months later, would often deliberately avoid meeting you in temple or socially elsewhere—clearly embarrassed for having revealed ultra-personal bedside confidences to a perfect stranger or even to their own rabbi. That I had once been privy to their innermost weakness, confusion, and inadequacy was just too much for them to manage.

In pastoral calling, whether in the hospital or at home, what never ceased to infuriate me more than anything else was when a doctor made it candidly clear to a critically or terminally ill member that all hope was gone! I still remember, early on in my young career, the day when I came into a member's hospital room to pay a call upon a middle-aged woman who just recently had been operated on for ovarian cancer. Her husband had confided to me beforehand that his wife was unaware how critically sick she was. "She's a fighter, Rabbi. She's determined to win this battle. She'll *never* give up or throw in the towel unless her doctor tells her that the battle is hopeless. It probably is, Rabbi. But without her hanging on to hope of *any* kind, she'll just flat out give up the fight."

When I called upon this woman, I found her shaken and sobbing. When she saw me, she blurted out: "Rabbi, I'm going to die!" She grabbed my hands and wept uncontrollably. I said to her, "Miriam, who told you that?" Through her sobbing she told me, "My doctor came in this morning and told me that the X-rays look bad. The cancer has spread widely and things look grim. It's over, Rabbi! Now I know I'm gonna die. No use fighting any more." She fell back upon her pillow and wept in despair.

I was beside myself with helplessness and utterly furious with her doctor. Even if his diagnosis was medically accurate, he should have realized that once he told her, in effect, that her cancer had ominously spread, and there was little or no chance that it would reverse itself, she would be astute enough to sense the inevitable and "prepare" herself for death.

This grim scene with Miriam confronted me at the very beginning of my rabbinate, when I had little experience coping with terminally ill patients and how doctors deal with their patients in reacting to bad news in general and fatal illness in particular. With my career now well behind me, I am even more convinced than ever, in my mind and heart, that doctors who feel under some professional pressure or mandate to share completely hopeless medical news or doomsday predictions with their patients become, in effect, instant executioners in the eyes of the patient. Far too many doctors, in my experience, still honestly believe that the patient's right to know must take precedence over dispensing false and illusory hope. With the right to know, the reasoning goes, the patient should be better able to set his or her mortal house in order and more realistically confront the end of life with infinitely more dignity, order, and peace.

I must admit that over the years of my pastoral calling, I have met a handful of men and women who earnestly and even unemotionally demanded that their doctors completely level with them about their grave condition. ("How much time, doc, do I really have left? I want to know without any ifs, ands, or bullshit. I can take it. Give it to me straight.")

I've stood at many a bedside listening to this kind of challenge flung at the doctor. The reality was, however, that only a minuscule number of patients who militantly insisted upon knowing the medical facts were able to face them unblinkingly and dispassionately. Far more demanded the truth and then were shattered and broken upon hearing the facts! They thought they could handle it, but they really couldn't and didn't.

Most physicians in my growing up and those I came into contact with in my early professional rounds rarely if ever felt impelled to share the darkest medical scenarios with their patients. Most physicians of a generation ago seemed to understand, intuitively and humanely, that the average patient would probably instantly crumble, emotionally, psychologically, and spiritually, if the bald, grim medical facts were given to them straight. Not only that, but upon learning the bitter medical truth, I've seen the will to fight of too many patients smashed outright and the doctor-patient relationship irretrievably damaged or permanently severed. The same was also sadly true for the patient's family and closest friends, whose heretofore-comforting support and strengthening presence in behalf of the patient now mattered pitiably little any more.

In the generation we live in today, I note sadly and despairingly that more and more young doctors, in their physical demeanor and conversation, coldly approach their patients as mere charts and X-rays. Simple humanity and visible caring for each patient— what we quite simply but meaningfully call in our Jewish tradition "menschlikeit"—is pathetically missing. Many doctors attempt to place the blame for the insensitivity and indifference of their manner on the larger medical system of today, which, they argue, has turned them into lackeys for the managed health care overlords who seem to have their cost-cutting administrative eyes focused only upon the cold financial bottom line.

From gods to flunkies in barely a generation! While the twenty-first century will undoubtedly reverse this shocking 180-degree shift in stature and control in the medical profession at large, there really is no certain expectation that patients can confidently look forward to medical practitioners who, by training and instinct, will daily mouth and live by an old Tibetan medical creed: "Through my contemplating the suffering I see daily in my work, I must move heaven and earth to increase my compassion and put kindness before all else."

The Christophers put it in an equally humanist way: "Help me to listen to my patients, diagnose carefully, prescribe conscientiously, and follow through faithfully. Teach me to blend gentleness with skill, to be a doctor with a *heart* as well as with a head."

In our Jewish tradition, the twelfth-century philosopher-physician Moses Maimonides challenged each new generation of doctors to recite each and every day of their medical career: "Inspire me, O God, with love for Thy creatures. In the sufferer, let me see only the human being. Do not allow thirst for profit, and ambition for renown to interfere with my profession. Never allow the thought to arise in me that I have attained sufficient knowledge, but vouchsafe to me the strength, the leisure, and the ambition ever to extend my horizons and my heart."

5

They Don't Make Rebbitzens
Like That Any More!
(or, The Vanishing Rabbi's Wife)

When the president of my sisterhood called me many years ago wanting to know what was up with my new assistant rabbi's wife, I knew she was on the warpath.

"Would you believe, Rabbi," fumed the sixty-eight-year-old sisterhood leader, "when I politely and graciously phoned to offer her the honor of pouring tea at our opening sisterhood program of the season, she shot back at me: `Does the sisterhood in this temple ever offer this tea-serving honor to a man, your own husband, perhaps, or any other male in the congregation?'

"Rabbi, I couldn't believe my ears! I told her that the women of our historic congregation have always felt that it was a very special honor to be invited to perform this sisterhood ritual. Would you believe, Rabbi, this young rebbitzen actually turned the honor down? She snippily told me that she was part of a new generation of women, which includes most rabbis' wives, who frown upon females only being considered for such public duties.

"Rabbi, when you interviewed your new assistant, did you have any inkling that he had a rebbitzen like that?"

I, of course, keenly understood that this young woman was part and parcel of a whole new generation who were excitingly and understandably caught up in the feminist movement.

They are very properly upset about the dismal and shameful second-class status of women in our male-dominated society. They were determined, some ferociously and "in your face," others more quiet and dignified but no less determined, to pull down the walls of sexual discrimination in our society, which they believed were a shameful affront to their womanhood and which they would tolerate no longer. I further reminded this sisterhood leader that her own daughter and both of my daughters were in full sympathy with these stirrings that were now shot through our entire culture. I am quite certain that I did not persuade my sisterhood leader one whit to open up her mind and heart as to what this young rabbi's wife objected to.

With my first assistant's wife, who had been with the temple family for several years, and who was cut out of far more traditional rebbitzen cloth, the long practiced and traditionally accepted duties, such as pouring tea and many other public life functions associated with the position of a minister's wife, were routinely embraced and performed without question or disdain.

I must confess that I was not completely taken by surprise when this incident with the sisterhood occurred. When I first interviewed this young woman's husband for the assistant-rabbi position, it was the usual one-on-one interview with the senior rabbi in tandem with the president of the congregation and the newly ordained rabbi. The first interview always took place on the campus of either our New York or Cincinnati school. Wives were never a part of the process. When the campus interview was deemed especially successful, the candidate was then invited to meet with the temple's search committee back home. At that time the candidate was generally accompanied by his wife. The second interview was conducted with the entire search committee and the senior rabbi. It was further arranged that a small subcommittee would meet separately with the young rebbitzen while the interview was going on. She would be shown around town and oriented in general as to the congregation and the community. There were also other opportunities for the couple to socialize with members of the committee.

With this particular assistant rabbi candidate, I went out of my way to arrange a private second dinner meeting with him and his wife before they visited the temple for the meeting with the search committee. I had sensed in our first interview, where I walked away from the meeting very high on him, that he might have an inner, unexpressed reservation about accepting the position. As it turned out, the young rabbi and his wife and I warmed up to each other famously over dinner and drinks, and I was frankly charmed with his lovely young wife. I sensed that she would fit in smoothly and capably with the larger temple family. At our dinner, no words about her strong feminist feelings or agenda passed between us. I sensed in her only a very strong and vital personality with a keen mind of her own who would appear to be first and foremost her own woman and, at the same time, a fine helpmate for her husband in our profession.

I never mentioned the contretemps with my sisterhood president to my young colleague's wife. As I got to know her better, I learned that growing up she had been very involved with women's rights organizations and feminist issues, which in the 1970s were beginning to shake up the sexual landscape in our country in many different professions and businesses. In 1972, for example, there was a major breakthrough in my own profession. The very first woman was ordained rabbi by our Reform seminary. By the end of the twentieth century, women rabbis were a major constituency in the Reform rabbinate and similarly in the Conservative and Reconstructionist movements. Fifty percent of the present day Reform rabbinical student body are women. The cantorial profession, which historically was also once an all-male profession, has in the Reform movement today become almost totally feminized. In the class of 1998, the School of Sacred Music invested eleven cantors, and nine of them were women. At present, a total of thirty-two students are studying for the Reform cantorate, of whom twenty-two are women.

The happiest spin-off surrounding the phenomenon of the disappearing rebbitzen in the rabbinate in this generation is that the wives (and now husbands as well) of rabbis are no longer frustratingly locked into demeaning and unfulfilling public roles. Until very recently, congregations engaging a rabbi routinely expected that the rabbinic spouse was automatically a "two-fer" part of the clerical package. The classic rebbitzen has always been a nonsalaried appendage of her husband who was automatically expected to assume a heavy load of public life duties whether she wanted to or not. Many rebbitzens rejoiced in these social responsibilities, and because of their intellectual and academic talent oftentimes played a major role in their congregations alongside their husbands.

Far more rebbitzens, however, were perfectly miserable in this essentially ancillary role. Many, if truth be told, were simply not cut out for public life. They had only married the rabbi and not the rabbinate. An even larger number of unhappy rebbitzens were profoundly ill at ease, if not resentful, that they were not able to pursue independent careers and jobs which they craved and were well qualified for. For me, it was a great joy to witness, in the latter part of my career, the young wives of my assistants being able to work totally independent of their husband's role in the congregation and the community. What resulted for them and others was infinitely greater happiness and fulfillment in their lives, in their marriages, and in the lives of their children.

The working rebbitzens of this generation have happily become part of all of the new and expanding feminist opportunities that are dramatically and positively reshaping and redefining the traditional feminine roles in our society. As far as the lay leadership and rank and file in the average congregation goes, most of them now rejoice in and take great pride in their rebbitzens' new freedom and new choices in the rabbinic family. A few of the sisterhood old-timers in the congregation, of course, are still around, resenting the shortage of rebbitzen-tea servers at temple events. However, I am confident that they will learn to direct their shock and scorn elsewhere in the courts of the Lord. Just think of their having to relate to the overall phenomenon of learning how to deal with women rabbis and cantors!

6

Rabbi, For a Long Time We've Been Growing Apart Translation: I'm Fooling Around with Somebody Else!
(or, The Challenge of Divorce Counseling)

In my post–World War II years at rabbinical school, the graduate school curriculum was understandably heavy with required and elective courses dealing with every facet of scholarly Jewish studies. What was almost totally omitted from the four (now five) years of rabbinical studies were any courses in marriage and divorce counseling—a major part of every rabbi's ministry. In my day, there was a part-time psychiatrist on the faculty who was available to meet privately with students who felt the need for professional counseling. The same psychiatrist also offered a minor elective in what was called "Human Relations" but few in the student body bothered to take it.

The august president of our seminary was the aging but still dynamic, internationally acclaimed rabbi and world Zionist leader, Dr. Stephen S. Wise. Once a week, on Thursday mornings, when he was not globe-trotting, he would meet with the junior and senior student body in his imposing study for a seminar loosely entitled "Problems in the Ministry." His seminars, however, rarely touched upon a single substantive matter of lay counseling. Most of the rabbinical students were serving student pulpits in the last three years of the rabbinical program and there was virtually no faculty member on hand to offer practical advice and counsel where desperately needed.

The charismatic Rabbi Wise's weekly seminars generally consisted of his sharing with us the final draft of his forthcoming Sunday morning sermon, which he delivered weekly from the make-shift congregational pulpit that had been transferred from the Free Synagogue building off Central Park West to New York City's illustrious Carnegie Hall. Because of the huge crowds flocking each week to hear Rabbi Wise, the congregation for decades had been renting Carnegie Hall for both Sunday and High Holy Day worship. We students, each Thursday morning, sat raptly at his feet in his study as he sonorously treated us to his customary headline-grabbing sermons.

Wise's sermon usually consumed most of the hour he set aside to be with "his boys." If there were a few minutes remaining before we were dismissed, on occasion he might ask us: "Well boys, what do you think?" Besides an occasional "brown-noser" in the class who felt impelled to rhapsodize over his sermon, the majority of us just sat there transfixed with awe and quietude. About the only truly practical bits of rabbinical advice he chose to share with us were: "When you feel yourself floundering with your sermon and losing your audience, just pound the pulpit harder with your fist!" "Make sure you relieve yourself before ascending the altar!" and "Never forget that there are fewer and fewer shmucks out there in the pews in this generation listening to you. Many of your congregants hold even more prestigious academic and professional credentials than your own!" This, above all: "The listening mind can only absorb what the ass will allow!"

Without demeaning any of Rabbi Wise's pulpit advice, come ordination we were all still babes in the woods when it came to honing specific counseling skills. A few of us were fortunate enough to have taken some elementary psych and social work courses while attending college before entering rabbinical school, and this gave us a modest professional advantage over the majority of our rabbinical classmates who had never been exposed to courses of this nature. At best, however, in the early years of our first congregational counseling experiences we young rabbis were forced to rely heavily on our instinctive ability to be compassionate listeners and strictly amateur problem-solvers flying by the seat of our clerical pants.

When the chips were down, we had to be brutally honest with ourselves and humbly acknowledge our personal and professional limitations in dealing with really complex and dysfunctional family dynamics. It behooved most of us young professionals to be astute enough to turn our congregants, where necessary, over to the real professionals in the counseling field. What saved many of us from doing irreparable harm to those who came to us in deep psychological trouble was the fact that hardly a rabbinic colleague in our profession when I first started out a half-century ago—and I'm certain in this generation today—did not have on hand a critical short list of psychiatrists, psychologists, and marriage counselors who were infinitely better qualified to step in and be available when necessary to take over this serious counseling responsibility.

Obviously, there are many counseling situations which a mature, skillful, and sensitive rabbi can tackle successfully without benefit of nonrabbinical professional help, particularly in counseling situations where specifically Jewish knowledge and moral and religious guidance is called for. Many times, however, we rabbis faced another depressing dilemma. Oftentimes, in our rabbinical career, we would refer a congregant to a psychiatrist, and after long-term professional therapy the congregant was worse off than before in both mind and wallet. In checking through the rabbinical curriculum catalogue of the present, I note that there are more specific courses in the field of human relations, but considering how much pastoral time engages the average rabbi, I still question how professionally prepared our young colleagues of today are for this highly complex and challenging responsibility.

The title of this chapter, referring to the whole subject of marital counseling, is a case in point. During the first few years of my rabbinate, when members sought me out for marriage counseling, my general procedure was to meet with the couple together at the very first session to get a preliminary overview of the problem. Then I would schedule successive meetings separately with the husband and the wife to get a more rounded feel of their personal and individual impressions as to what was wrong with the marriage, and try to discover ways out of the dilemma. Then I would set up a "summit" meeting for the three of us where I would summarize for the two of them my own rabbinical understanding of what each had shared with me about what they felt was wrong and damaging with the marriage. If my "take" was on target, then in the sessions to follow we would explore together how the marriage might be salvaged—assuming it could be salvaged. At times I would return to the one-on-one session with each party when my gut told me that I was still not getting the whole story. The biggest challenge was to determine how much mutual respect remained in the marriage. Once it became painfully obvious that the partners had lost total respect for one another—not to mention love—I was ready to conclude that the marriage was virtually over and that divorce was inevitable, even if one party was desperate for it to continue no matter what the human cost might be.

In the very early years of my rabbinic counseling, due to my prior lack of professional training in this field, I was often buffaloed, more often by husbands than wives, into swallowing whole the rationalizations being offered to explain why the unhappy spouse was deriving little happiness or fulfillment from the marriage. The long and short of it, as I was soon to discover, was that I was being unashamedly lied to! Sometimes, it took many wasted and basically dishonest sessions before the real truth emerged and the spouse would embarrassingly confess that he was flagrantly fooling around with someone else, or that he was in an adulterous relationship with another party which had been going on for ages. Before this was factually put on the counseling table, I was usually treated to every phony reason but the real one as to who was essentially to blame for the marital break-up.

One particular counseling case finally ended my youthful rabbinical naiveté. I had long suspected that the husband was playing around and was covering up his sordid infidelities by voicing all kinds of bitter complaints to me about his wife's failure to "grow with him culturally and socially." Sometimes he would make snide comments describing her basic slovenliness in their home life, her carelessness in dress, her being a lousy mother, or her indifference to his sexual needs. This litany of complaints was endless and unforgiving. Finally, I could take it no longer and challenged him point-blank, "Is there another woman in your life? And how long have you been cheating on your wife?"

After red-faced hemming and hawing for a moment, the truth finally came out. I was fit to be tied. "Why the hell didn't you tell me this at our first private session? All we've been doing for these many counseling sessions is just spinning our counseling wheels! I'm not here to sit in judgment upon your infidelity. But the gross lies and deceptions about your wife—that's utterly intolerable, despicable, and unforgivable!" From that counseling session on—and I thank God it came early on in my career—with every couple who sought me out for marital counseling, the very *first* question I threw directly at both parties was, "Tell me straight out, is there another person now in your life with whom you are romantically and sexually involved? If yes, the hurdles ahead for a possible reconciliation are probably bleak as hell, if not doomed. If no, we're still not out of the woods by a long shot; but at least we can now be brutally and yet compassionately honest and truthful enough with each other in trying to see whether this troubled and severely damaged marriage has any honest and realistic chance of being salvaged."

Failing to nail down the "obvious," of course, was only one of the many frustrations in marriage counseling. Equally exasperating was the painful awareness that in far too many situations the average couple in trouble with their marriage would turn to the rabbi as the *last* resort. That is to say, couples would often come to see me and my colleagues far too late in the process. By the time one or the other spouse contacted me for help, they had either reached the point of absolute no return in their marriage, or they had toyed with some ineffectual long-term marriage counselors, or they were knee-deep in divorce lawyers, all too often dismally indifferent to conciliation efforts and solely focusing on bitter custody battles and dividing up the fiscal assets. Somewhere along the line, a hysterical parent, grandparent, or friend would beg the distraught couple to turn to the rabbi. One last stab!

Even if the couple had made the judgment call to seek me out first rather than last, there was still no guarantee that the outcome would have been any different. Pitiable timing often wasted everybody's involvement. As I look back now at near-ly a half-century of rabbinic marriage counseling, my personal track record in getting couples to reconcile with each other where there were truly salvageable factors involved—and when they were able to connect with me early on amidst their tensions and frictions—included more successes then failures.

What helped me immeasurably—and this could well be the long-range effective counseling technique for all clergymen to consider—was my practice of planting the seed of future marital counseling in the hearts and minds of all young couples when they came to me for the first premarital interview. As I have discussed in another chapter, whether one is a rabbi, minister, or priest, we clergy miss the boat completely unless we deal with the inevitable realities of marital tensions *before* marriage. It is imperative to alert couples early on, way before the ceremony, and let each of them know that your counseling door and professional ear will always be available long after the wedding has taken place. My most gratifying calls are those that I have received over my career from couples I married and who feel close enough to have me reenter their lives in times of crisis. This in no way means that I believe that every marriage in serious trouble is salvageable. That is why divorce was wisely sanctioned early on in Jewish history. The chances of mending a broken marriage, however, are vastly enhanced if the timing factor is operative, the right counselor is available, and enough love and respect still remain in the relationship, so that, while seriously frayed and flawed, it is still potentially redeemable.

7

Great House Tonight, Rabbi
(or, The High Holy Day Trauma)

At the beginning of every academic year at rabbinical school, each seminarian is assigned a student pulpit for the High Holy Days somewhere around the country. When the Hebrew Union College–Jewish Institute of Religion became a five-year course of graduate studies (it was originally four years), it ultimately mandated that the first year be spent living and studying in Israel at the Jerusalem School. All rabbinical students become eligible for High Holy Day assignments in their sophomore graduate school year. Every year thereafter, the student rabbis are generally assigned to a new and different Jewish community for the ten-day High Holy Day period. Though a half-century has passed, I still vividly remember each one of my awesome student experiences—the first in Lynchburg, Virginia; then in Saranack Lake, New York; and finally in Brooklyn, New York.

These Rosh Hashanah and Yom Kippur student pulpit experiences were particularly exciting because, as very young graduate students, we were suddenly catapulted from our humble role as seminary neophytes into visiting rabbinic dignitaries who became overnight community celebrities in all of these tiny and far-flung Jewish communities which were too small and scattered to support a full-time rabbi throughout the year. It was very heady stuff to cope with, even for the most

53

mature incipient rabbi. After these adrenalin-elevating High Holy Day pulpit experiences came to a quick end after Yom Kippur, it was not easy to slip back into classroom student anonymity where most of the professors treated us as juvenile cheder smart-asses.

My own three student High Holy Day pulpits on the East Coast were a bit larger than the average small congregation elsewhere. Where these sparsely populated Jewish communities boasted a slightly larger number of permanent Jewish residents, many of the rabbinical students in Cincinnati and New York were required to serve these High Holy Day communities as student rabbis once a month throughout the entire academic year, thereby gaining invaluable and ongoing student rabbinical experience before ordination.

I attended the New York branch of HUC-JIR right after World War II, where I served as a cryptographer in the Army signal Corps overseas in New Guinea, the Philippines, and Japan. The American Reform movement in 1947 was in the midst of a vast explosion of new congregations in the Greater New York suburban area. Many of my rabbinical classmates in Manhattan were regularly called upon, beyond the freshman year, to serve these infant congregations on a weekly basis. This oftentimes took valuable learning time away from their seminary studies. However, by ordination time, most of the student rabbis at our New York School had full-time positions waiting for them in the burgeoning suburban congregations they led in their student years.

In my years of rabbinical school in New York, I opted only for the annual High Holy Day position, deliberately refraining from servicing a new congregation whether monthly or weekly throughout the academic year. Fortunately, since I was still single and living at home, I did not need the extra income these student pulpits invitingly offered to many of my married classmates. I preferred to devote full-time to my rabbinical studies without any of the burdensome distractions and extra congregational pressures that a student pulpit imposed upon my classmates.

I must admit, however, that I always looked forward to luxuriating in my High Holy Day student experience. It gave me and all of my classmates a delicious, exciting, and ego-elevating very first taste of what the holy days and synagogue life in general, with all of their unbelievable pressures and pleasures, were going to be like for the rest of our careers. In the long run, places like Lynchburg and Saranack Lake, despite the relatively small size of their High Holy Day Jewish constituencies, proved to be not so different from the three major congregations I was eventually called upon to serve in the years ahead.

Two of the congregations where I served as assistant rabbi and then later as senior rabbi were old-line classical Reform synagogue behemoths founded in the mid-nineteenth century in Pittsburgh and in Hartford. The third congregation was an exploding brand-new suburban congregation in the Mount Lebanon suburb of Pittsburgh.

What made these two full-time, year-round congregations and the part-time High Holy Day congregations very same in my mind was that the synagogue crowd ambience, behavior, expectations, and attitudes differed very little whether the institution was large or small. With every assistant rabbi who served with me over the years in my last New England pulpit, I remember telling them all when they came under my wing fresh from ordination: "No matter what frustrating and teeth-grinding situations and people you are inevitably going to run into here in West Hartford, on or off the board of trustees or in the community at large, you can invariably count on confronting these same difficult types of Jews in congregations large or small in the whole length and breadth of the American Jewish community." The one, major consoling factor, however, I made sure to remind them, was that there would also and always be a small but inspired cadre of perfectly marvelous lay leaders and rank-and-file members who would more than make up for the obnoxious and ever present synagogue and community types they would have to put up with in this strangest, wildest, and yet most wonderful of all professions.

My very first post-ordination congregation was in Pittsburgh. I was assistant rabbi to one of the legendary great rabbis, scholars, and incomparable preachers of the twentieth-century American Jewish community, Dr. Solomon B. Freehof of Rodef Shalom Temple.

Despite the congregation's vast membership of twenty-one hundred families in 1951, compared with the paltry hundred individual Jews who had made up my first student pulpit in Lynchburg, the basic crowd make-up and general congregational attitudes, behavior, and motivations were remarkably the same.

Both congregations were faced with the same daunting seating problem. The High Holy Day handful of Jews in Lynchburg were barely able to squeeze into their modest little synagogue building in town. Because of the utterly huge temple membership in Pittsburgh, the congregation each year was forced to rent the neighboring, massive Syria Mosque Shrine building, which for many years housed the Pittsburgh Symphony Orchestra. The temple's magnificent Byzantine main sanctuary, built in 1906, had a seating capacity of fourteen hundred people which barely accommodated less than a third of the temple's High Holiday membership needs. To accommodate these vast hordes, the temple for years had to run a parallel High Holy Day worship service at the Mosque, where more than twenty-five hundred other members were seated for holy day services. To make sure that the Syria Mosque members did not feel cheated by having to worship outside the temple sanctuary, the senior rabbi and I rotated our rabbinical presence in the evening and morning at both places. The system worked amazingly well for over a generation and more, until temple membership fell off dramatically in the last couple of decades, and now the entire congregation can be accommodated in one sitting in the temple sanctuary.

For a freshly ordained young rabbi to step out onto this vast Carnegie Hall–like concert stage, temporarily converted into a synagogue altar with makeshift Holy Ark, banks of gorgeous flowers and pulpit chairs, facing a virtually jam-packed High Holy Day audience of twenty-five hundred worshippers at night, then another fourteen hundred worshippers at the temple in the morning, this absolutely took my breath away!

It was not too long, however, before I realized that whether I was conducting worship in the Lilliputian Lynchburg synagogue or in the major metropolis of Pittsburgh, both of these Reform Jewish congregations were there for the same noble and ignoble High Holy day needs, expectations, and impact. The "nobilities" surrounding Jews at worship during the High Holy Days were obvious and inspiring to both clergy and laity. Who would not be deeply moved at this annual eye-popping spectacle of committed and uncommitted Jews flocking en masse to the synagogue in mind-boggling droves to pay honor to their religion, even if only twice a year! Christian America, of course, was similarly caught up in the comparable Christmas–Easter holy day syndrome, when the churches, like the synagogues, were overwhelmed twice a year with the faithful and not so faithful, and with hardly an empty pew to be found.

Here, however, the comparison ends. Whether in mid-twentieth-century America, when I began my rabbinate, or today, fifty years later as we move into the twenty-first century, affiliated American Protestants and Catholics proportionally are still the same as American Jews when it comes to daily and weekly worship habits. It is no secret that only Orthodox Jews, who represent a bare 10 percent of American Jews, boast an amazingly high year-round percentage of daily and Sabbath worshippers as well as regular worshipping in their synagogues for every other major and minor holy day in the

Jewish calendar. In Reform and Conservative Jewish congre-gations, which make up the vast majority of affiliated American Jews, barely 10 percent of the congregational mem-bership attends weekly or on any other Jewish holiday wor-ship. "Special event" Sabbaths, of course, will periodically exceed the 10 percent level of regulars, but not by much. The bottom line is that for non-Orthodox American Jews, regular worship is still a very low priority—the only exception being on the High Holy Days. Student rabbis sense this phenomenon very early on in their pre-ordination seasonal pulpits, and many years after ordination, in congregations large or small, it never really gets any better.

Rabbis quickly learn that there are basically only two cop-ing mechanisms by which they can handle the depressing real-ity of twice-a-year congregational attendance. The first is to burn up with righteous indignation and proceed sermonically to bawl the hell out of your people for their pitiful worship habits. Sarcasm thus often becomes the key preaching mood of the holy days. The laying on of mass guilt flows acidly from pulpit to squirming pew.

A second coping mechanism, however, takes a radically different, maturer, and far more positive pulpit tack. This wiser and infinitely more productive rabbinic approach to the seasonal Jewish full-house syndrome goes, more shrewdly, something like this: As a rabbi, I have only four pulpit shots at my people during the evening and morning of Rosh Hashanah and Yom Kippur. Either I choose to waste my time belittling my people's basic motivation for coming to worship once a year, or I'm going to try and move heaven and earth in my preaching and praying power to have my congregants focus, even if only for one inspired moment, upon the more immedi-ate, deeper, and nobler challenge of the holy days. Even if this once-a-year mob manages to experience only a momentary "high," it is a far, far worthier accomplishment to try spiritual-ly to elevate them rather than to childishly pout and settle for a tempting but basically demeaning pulpit cheap shot which, in reality, accomplishes nothing.

The smart young rabbi who latches on quickly, in his or her career, to this second High Holy Day coping mechanism will confront the holy days with far less angst, cynicism, and despair. Firing your members up rather than snidely dragging them down can, more often than not, achieve the central purpose and timeless challenge of these lofty though fleeting sacred milestones of our faith. Thus, what essentially makes the seasonal house great is not its impressive size but its inspired expectations.

For us clergy, there is no more stressful challenge than the period of the High Holy Days. What with the intoxicating mob scene, the logistics alone can almost wipe us rabbis out! It's not just the relentless pressure of deciding weeks and months in advance what to preach about before such packed houses. As the years go by in my profession, pulpit preparation remains a ceaselessly daunting task. Finding the perfect sermon mix between the topical and the eternal is a never-ending preaching challenge. Where and when to resort to crowd-pleasing humor and guaranteed storytelling dramatics unendingly tests the preacher's skill and respect for the audience.

Surrounding the annual preaching pressures are the thousand and one behind-the-scenes rabbinic logistic preparations for the worship service, such as inviting key lay people for holy day pulpit reading honors, a task always carried out in full awareness that one or two self-important nonentities in the congregation will inevitably be overlooked in the frenzy and proceed to hold a grudge against you for another year. Then there are the pre–Rosh Hashanah professional-staff road-mapping sessions with the rabbi, assistant rabbi, cantor, and choir director, all creatively seeking to fit into their appointed prayer book and altar slots. When you add to all of this the inevitable synagogue-office madhouse occurring just outside your study, where you have to deal with members in good standing and others in annual deadbeat financial standing besieging the temple office for last-minute seats for additional family and out-of-town guests coming to worship. Not to be overlooked are the frenzied D-Day preparations on the part of ushers, maintenance personnel, and police security to see to it that peak crowd and traffic control is managed with appropriate smoothness and dignity.

In the gargantuan congregations that I was privileged to serve, coordinating the highly complicated High Holy Day scenario was always a superhuman logistical achievement for the entire synagogue family. It often made me and, I am certain, many of my colleagues long for the graveyard quietude and spiritual simplicity of the year-round weekly Sabbath evening service setting, where the greatest excitement pertained to wondering what kind of schnecken would be served at the Oneg Shabbat reception.

It is so roguishly tempting for us rabbis, over the years, to become somewhat cynical about the long-term and even short-term religious impact of the High Holy Day season upon our people. On balance, as I think back over my career, there is appreciably more positive than negative here. I have always had a very low religious tolerance for the kind of lay mentality that reacts to the annual phenomenon of the Rosh Hashanah and Yom Kippur synagogue "full house" as an impressive "achievement" in Jewish life and identity. On one level, even rabbis cannot argue with success. Were Jews of every conceivable motivation or denomination to forgo coming to the synagogue even only once a year, affiliated and even unaffiliated American Judaism would be in far worse shape then it is.

The High Holy Days numbers game, however, is not the central issue. The commanding factor, which is at heart a never-ending mystery, is that both rabbis and laity continue to remain in the dark about how to satisfactorily explain the High Holy Days compulsion of the majority of basically indifferent and uncommitted Jews just to show up.

Many of my colleagues attribute the jam-packed High Holy Days syndrome to simple lay guilt and leave it at that. I have never been completely comfortable with so simplistic an explanation. Guilt, after all, assumes a bad conscience. Guilt assumes expectation of punishment. The fact of the matter is that the multitudes of non-traditional modern Jews operate with little or no shame. Nor do most modern-day Jews fear divine disfavor when it comes to ignoring public worship once a week or even once a year.

What I truly believe impels our laity, at this unique time of the year, to make their annual High Holy Day pilgrimage is nothing more complex than the fact that Rosh Hashanah and Yom Kippur constitute for the masses an impressive, milestone *social* occasion, akin to a joyous birthday or anniversary or reunion where all the members of the extended family are simply eager to be with one other to celebrate the familial and religious ties that bind and elevate us all.

The purely social pull that motivates the family to include the synagogue in its outreach is not to be sneered at. For within the social embrace of the generations at the time of the holy day season at home and in the synagogue, important, meaningful attention is paid, albeit briefly, to the central spiritual purpose and challenge of the holidays. The deep thoughts and provocative challenges directed at Jews at this special time of the Jewish year still arouse us all, whether we choose to admit it or not, to try and renew the world by renewing ourselves morally and spiritually. This will always remain the exclusive focus of Rosh Hashanah and Yom Kippur.

Cynics may well wonder whether this annual shot of "instant Judaism" will have a significant impact upon the average High Holy Day Jew. To be brutally honest, there is probably very little of sustaining meaning and impact. Rabbis, however, sell themselves, their people, and Judaism short if they just waste their pulpit time in condemning the mystifying mass presence of the High Holy Day congregation. Ours, in reality, is not to condemn. Ours is rather to move heaven and earth to try and draw as many of our people as we can infinitely closer to God and to their heritage through the very best of our sermons, liturgy, and music. Pulpit scolding may temporarily relieve rabbinic frustration. But it does little or nothing to rouse the High Holy Day masses—no matter why they are there—to a soaringly higher and deeper awareness of the ultimate reason why they are there, and of what they are, in essence, ideally called upon to do and to be.

8

Rabbi, You're Driving Them Away from Judaism

(or, Who Is Really at Fault?)

Whenever a parent in my congregation or a nonmember called me or came to my study to discuss a pending marriage in the family, the tip-off that the marriage in question was an interfaith marriage usually came when the conversation began: "Rabbi, our son, Jeffrey, has met this *wonderful* girl! And, we *love* her! She's beautiful, warm, friendly, and has a marvelous academic background to match his, and they seem to make a perfect fit. We *love* her, Rabbi; but, there's *one* problem. Kathy's not Jewish. She's not much of a Christian either, Rabbi. Doesn't ever go to church. She doesn't believe in Jesus. But, Rabbi, she told Jeffrey that she's more than willing to raise the children Jewish! You will marry them, won't you?"

Throughout the years of my rabbinate, as soon as I heard this mantra, "We *love* her, Rabbi," or "We *love* him," I knew immediately that we were dealing here with a very sticky and tense intermarriage situation. And I further knew in my gut that the parent invariably and fervently wished that it were otherwise.

The members of the three congregations I served in my career always knew my uncompromising position *against* officiating at interfaith ceremonies. They were also aware of my very vocal and negative condemnation of my colleagues who chose to officiate at marriages between a Jew and an unconverted non-Jew. But that did not stop the telephone calls to my study or to my home from unaffiliated Jews who were either unaware of my feelings or who harbored the hope that if the couple agreed to raise their children Jewishly, I would then agree to officiate at their mixed marriage. (For purposes of clarity, I use the terms "interfaith marriage" and "mixed marriage" to designate a marriage between a Jew and an *un*converted non-Jew. Where both partners are Jewish, even if one of them is a convert, the marriage is fully recognized by Jewish law and the Jewish community as 100 percent Jewish.)

Ironically, when the average interfaith couple came into my study over the years for their very first meeting with me, and we began to delve into this thorny problem, more often than not I found that I had an easier time relating to the *non*-Jew than to the *born* Jew! Once the non-Jew got over the nervousness of meeting privately with a rabbi for the first time, he or she was invariably shocked to discover that I was a sympathetic ally of sorts. That is to say, instead of teaming up with the Jewish partner to pressure the non-Jew to convert to Judaism, lo and behold, the rabbi (at least this particular rabbi) was far more concerned with fully respecting the Christian partner's religious background. I would routinely ask whether the Christian was really prepared, emotionally and spiritually, to reject and abandon his or her religion. The non-Jew was also further amazed and vastly relieved to hear a rabbi candidly state that he was sensitive to the fact that even the most alienated Protestant or Catholic comes to an interfaith marriage or to conversion to Judaism before marriage with very mixed and troubled personal and family emotions of every kind. All the love in the world between an interfaith couple can never fully paper over or resolve the significant differences in religious background.

In premarital interview after interview, even when the non-Jew was ready and eager to go through a conversion before the marriage, I made it my business to remind the potential convert that at any future point in the long, educational process leading to conversion, he or she should feel perfectly free to back off or even to back out of the conversion altogether. Furthermore, I always said, if there were still any lingering, substantive doubts and reservations about taking the final vows after the conversion process was over, he or she should *not* go through the conversion ceremony. Any sensitive rabbi, I said reassuringly, would fully endorse and respect a decision to halt the process.

The removal of this conversion pressure, up and down the line, is a factor of great importance for the average convert candidate. Many a Jewish partner, unfortunately, tends to ignore if not dismiss this conscious or unconscious pressure. Nine-tenths of the convert candidates whom I personally led through the conversion study process went on, willingly and joyously, through the final conversion ceremony. However, every once in a while a candidate would choose to stop short at the end and would confess to me an unwillingness to go through conversion. For the first time in their lives, some would confide, they had discovered that their Christian upbringing still resonated deeply in mind and heart. They just could not bring themselves finally to give up Christ! The intensive learning about Judaism in the conversion course studies had only reaffirmed this deep emotional and spiritual attachment to Christianity. They still, of course, dearly loved their Jewish partner. They still wanted to get married, notwithstanding the many basic religious differences. But, they were not ready to or willing to *fully* embrace Judaism. Perhaps at some later time. Perhaps never.

Whenever a wavering convert shared such honest and fervent gut feelings with me, I simply but admiringly congratulated him or her. More than that, I applauded the courage that it took to halt the process at that climactic moment. Absolutely nothing had been lost, I said. At best, they had received a marvelous Jewish education that would enable them to cope more realistically with their partner's Jewish background. At worst, both partners now more clearly realized where they really stood with each other's religious identities and how these differences could adversely affect their marriage. The key issue now should be the more immediate decision as to whether their marriage should ever take place.

I mentioned above that at the first premarital meeting I often found myself more sympathetic with the non-Jew than with the Jew. In far too many cases over the years, it quickly became apparent that some Jewish partners in the interfaith relationship—interestingly enough, more often men than women—looked upon themselves as casual bystanders in the conversion process. They apparently felt that their status as born Jews or as indifferently raised Jews, or even as completely alienated Jews, placed them in some sort of "spectator" status whereby their own personal attachment to Judaism was looked upon as peripheral at best. For many of these totally marginal Jews, their exclusive motivation for having a rabbi marry them, they freely admitted, was to placate a hysterical, guilt-ridden Jewish parent or grandparent. Their family, they openly admitted, would be far less embarrassed or mortified if a rabbi were to unite the interfaith couple in marriage.

All that such minimalist Jews really craved was a Jewish "look" for the ceremony! They would implore the rabbi who was willing to officiate at mixed marriages simply to Jewishly "dress-up" the ceremonies with the historical Jewish wedding rituals—having the interfaith couple, for example, stand together under a chuppah (the wedding canopy), reciting the traditional marital wedding vows, drinking together from the Kiddush wedding goblet, and smashing a glass under heel to cap this faux Jewish wedding ceremony. It was clearly "faux" in the sense that, despite the highly visible inclusion of all the traditional Jewish wedding rituals in the world, which were often superficially co-opted for such public ceremonies, when the chips were down, no truly self-respecting Jew or any perceptive non-Jew, and least of all no responsible rabbi, could ever be under any illusion that such slapped-together wedding ceremonies were ever to be viewed as *legitimately* Jewish or as faithfully promoting *authentic* Jewish commitment and loyalty.

Mixed-marriage ceremonies, of course, are *legally* valid. They are just not *Jewishly* valid, as the ceremonial exchange-of-rings phrase puts it: "according to the laws of Moses and the faith of Judaism." By the same token, whenever a rabbi co-officiates with a Protestant minister or a Catholic priest, it is no secret that the religious comfort level on both sides of the aisle is jeopardized severely. Honest and practicing Catholics, Protestants, and Jews have confessed to me time and time again that they tended to squirm unbearably when obliged to witness this hodge-podge of cross-religious wedding rituals and traditions. Jew and non-Jew together instinctively sense that this type of ecumenical charade does no justice nor brings any honor to either Christianity or Judaism. To drastically lower the tension level on both sides of the family, I have always, throughout my career, energetically recommended a *civil* wedding ceremony for *all* mixed-married situations. The civil rites are honorable, dignified, and totally respected by all religions as legal and proper. What is more, neither side of the family attending a civil ceremony need ever feel that their religious traditions and background are being deliberately affronted or compromised.

Sadly, what far too many Jews and non-Jews fail to understand about the Jewish wedding ceremony is the specific nature of the *rabbi's* authentic role and prime responsibility in Jewish marriage officiation. The rabbi, according to Jewish law and tradition, does not actually "marry" the couple. In a normal Jewish wedding ceremony, the couple marry each other according to the historical rites and commitments of the Jewish faith. The rabbi traditionally only acts as an "arranger" or "facilitator," or as it is known in Hebrew, a *mesadder kiddushin.* In other words, *my* prime rabbinic function is to represent the

Jewish community and the religion of Judaism by publicly witnessing and validating the vows of a Jewish man and a Jewish woman who are pledging together to unite their Jewish lives in a sacred Jewish marriage. Standing before me, as the rabbi, the couple are committing themselves to perpetuate the best of Jewish religious values and practices in their married life ahead. Obviously, if one partner in this relationship is not Jewish, the marriage, in the eyes of Judaism and the Jewish community, is not Jewish, despite the presence of a rabbi at the ceremony and any and all of the Jewish ritualistic trimmings thrown in. In a word, a rabbi should never be there for "show." A rabbi, incidentally, should also not be there for the dough, although many "Marryin' Sams" unscrupulously exact scandalously high fees for such interfaith officiating shams.

I should add, however, that not every rabbi who officiates at interfaith ceremonies is to be lumped together with the Marrying Sams or Samanthas in our profession. While the majority of my Reform colleagues in the Central Conference of American Rabbis still refuse to officiate at mixed marriages, and have publicly affirmed and reaffirmed their opposition three times during the course of the twentieth century, there is still a minority group of respected colleagues who allow themselves to officiate if they can exact a sincere pledge from the mixed-marital couple. The pledge, oral or written, has the couple enroll in a substantive conversion course before marriage, and agree to raise their children Jewishly and affiliate with a congregation. The hope here is that the non-Jewish partner will one day embrace Judaism formally.

Colleagues who insist upon these basic conditions for their interfaith rabbinic officiating where the non-Jew chooses to forgo formal conversion to Judaism before marriage, genuinely believe that this kind of rabbinical outreach to the mixed-marital couple will eventually keep the couple within the embrace of the Jewish community. With the alarmingly high intermarriage rate in this country—over 50 percent at present and growing—some of my colleagues feel that every possible door in the Jewish community, rabbinic and lay, should be left wide-open and inviting to every mixed-marital couple. Many frustrated and guilt-ridden Jewish parents whose children are caught up in the intermarriage dilemma are more than willing to scrap even these minimum conditions of intent and promise for their non-Jewish future sons and daughters-in-law. If the kids want to get married, they argue, whether parents like it or not, no rabbi should be permitted to drive them away from Judaism, and no agency or institution in the Jewish community should turn the couple off.

All rabbis—those who officiate and those who do not—are confronted with a new and ominous wrinkle in modern Jewish life. Many find themselves "under the gun" in many congregations from temple lay leaders and members at large who demand that *all* rabbis be infinitely more accommodating and lenient in this matter of rabbinic officiation. More and more congregations, when interviewing for rabbis, make no bones about rejecting candidates out of hand who do not agree in advance to officiate at mixed marriages, even though such demands are roundly denounced by the placement committee of the Reform rabbinate.

Rabbis who waive conversion as a precondition for the non-Jew to be married Jewishly are only, I believe, pitiably demonstrating to the non-Jew that Judaism makes little or no serious religious demands. Even where conversion actually takes place, rabbis well know that there is still no automatic guarantee of lifetime Jewish practice and fidelity. So much of this, in the last analysis, primarily hinges upon the sincere and continuing role-modeling of the *Jewish* partner. In my many decades of interfaith counseling, as I intimated before, I have had greater and more frustrating problems in dealing with the *Jewish* partner than with the non-Jewish partner. How many colleagues of mine have also endured the perfectly distasteful experience of confronting a rash of born and ill-bred Jews who insist upon putting heavy pressure on their non-Jewish mates to become Jewish despite no Jewish conviction or religious passion of their own. In far too many cases, Jewish parental pressure is the sole motivating force cajoling or demanding conversion before marriage. In far too many initial conferences with the interfaith couple, I soon sensed a frivolous nonchalance or, what was even worse, a basic disdain emanating from the Jewish partner regarding his or her lack of commitment to Judaism.

I must also confess that when confronting these Jewishly lackadaisical types, I have many times lost my rabbinical cool. I often proceeded to dress down the born and indifferent Jew. I have reminded such Jewishly uncommitted and sometimes even hostile types that if they have no truly honest intention at this decisive religious crossroads in their lives to commit themselves *totally* to their own Jewish faith, and pledge solemnly to actively role-model Jewishly for their non-Jewish mate in the marriage ahead, then they really have no right whatsoever to pressure the non-Jew to convert to Judaism! I tell them that it is pure hypocrisy for an uncommitted Jew to make such conversion demands upon the non-Jew.

So many times, I have sadly witnessed potential converts passionately craving to become Jewish and lead exemplary Jewish lives only to be faced with the shameful and heartbreaking realization that the Jewish partner didn't give a damn or was simply going through the motions, making a sad mockery of the whole conversion process—before, during and after. Frankly, unless I was successful in exacting a solemn promise from the Jewish partner to exemplify the best of Judaism in the couple's future Jewish life ahead, I often refused to meet with them any further. More and more of my colleagues, I believe, are woefully remiss in not bluntly reminding all interfaith couples—not to mention Jewish couples as well—that less and less attention should be focused upon *getting* married and more and more attention on *staying* married. While religious differences in marriage are only one factor among many others resulting in the shamefully high divorce rate in this country today, they remain alarmingly high on the list of overall marital friction and failure. Religious compatibility is no automatic guarantee of marital success. But at least minimally, it certainly does assure a joyous and inspired head-start which, if richly and creatively sustained and enlarged upon over the years, can become a powerful and sure-fire factor contributing to true marital success and fulfillment.

So who is really driving whom away from Judaism? As long as there are Jewish parents deluding themselves as to what constitutes getting married Jewishly, as long as there are interfaith couples choosing to live in a wasteland of religious indifference and make-believe, as long as there are rabbis prepared to sanction such indignities, Judaism and Jewish life will continue to be served ignobly by all parties concerned.

9

We're Planning a Las Vegas Night for Our Kid's Bar Mitzvah
(or, Making a Mockery of the Jewish Future)

The Reform Jewish movement has gone from one extreme to the other in its relationship to the ritual of Bar Mitzvah. Non-Reform Jews, unfamiliar with the history and development of Reform Judaism in the early nineteenth century in Germany, have unfairly criticized the reformers for unceremoniously dumping this historic thirteen-year-old male coming-of-age rite of passage. Getting rid of Bar Mitzvah, they charge, was but another sorry example of German Reform Judaism deliberately turning its back upon its traditional Jewish past. Critics of Reform further complain that its main motivation was merely to copy-cat Christian coming of age rituals as part of its assimilationist tendency. They argue, as well, that the clamor among the early Reform Jews for sermons in German, an updated prayer book liturgy, and the introduction of the organ into the synagogue are proof that the fledgling Reform movement was nothing more than scandalous escapism from Orthodoxy, which resulted in a watered-down if not bastardized version of traditional Judaism.

The winds of change created by the French Revolution and the Napoleonic sweep across Europe deeply affected the Jews of Western Europe. The walls of the ghetto were finally beginning to crumble, and a new generation of Jews were beginning to mainstream themselves into Christian European society. In no way, however, did the early Reform Jews seek to scrap their Jewish past. Their basic and sincere desire was to seek out ways and means of modernizing the historic faith and to make it more relevant and responsive to their new political freedoms and economic opportunities in Christian Western Europe.

If anything, the scrapping of the Bar Mitzvah ritual is a perfect example of how the faith was modernized by creating a radical and Jewishly positive educational and ceremonial opportunity for Jewish girls to come of age along with Jewish boys. Up to the emergence of nineteenth-century Reform Judaism, only young *men* received a full and formal Jewish education, which reached a ceremonial plateau of thirteen-year-old adolescent entry into young-adult Jewish life through the vehicle of the Bar Mitzvah ritual in the synagogue. Reform Jews wanted young women to have co-equal Jewish educational opportunities and be privileged to have a comparable religious rite of passage whereby the adolescent Jewish woman could also be formally ushered into the young-adult Jewish community.

Nineteenth-century German Reform Jews, in search of a new coeducational religious coming of age vehicle, saw in the Christian Confirmation ritual beyond the ghetto a good religious model to emulate for their own educational and religious goals. While Catholic and Protestant Confirmation rites were generally offered to Christian boys and girls at a much younger age than thirteen, the German-Jewish reformers set thirteen for the new coeducational ceremony. The radical change they instituted was for Jewish boys and girls to begin their Jewish studies together at around five or six years of age in a weekly Sabbath or Sunday school setting. When boys and girls turned thirteen, upon successful completion of this early level of their Jewish studies, they were "formally" confirmed together into their faith on the holiday of Shavuot. This holiday was specifically chosen for the new rite of Jewish Confirmation because, according to ancient tradition, the Ten Commandments were given by God to Moses and the Jewish people on this very holy day. Thus it made dramatic sense to place Reform Confirmation on the very day when our ancestors at Mount Sinai affirmed and confirmed their faith in God and the covenant.

When the Reform movement came to the United States in the mid-nineteenth century, the Bar Mitzvah rite had totally disappeared from the Reform ritual. By the beginning of the twentieth century, the Confirmation ceremony which had replaced it was rescheduled to age fourteen and then, in time, was advanced to fifteen. This allowed teenage boys and girls to benefit from an additional two years of Jewish education before they were confirmed into their faith. After World War II, the overwhelming majority of Reform Jewish congregations arranged for Confirmation to take place at age sixteen, where it remains today. In the past generation, the Reform movement has developed eleventh- and twelfth-grade Jewish high school educational programs in the synagogue to further extend the Jewish educational process all the way from nursery school to the threshold of college.

Post–World War II American Reform Judaism saw an explosion of its congregational numbers. From a prewar 1940 constituency of about 250 congregations, the nationwide Reform movement tripled its numbers in the 1950s and 1960s. What was even more amazing to behold in this expansionary period was that East European Jews— mainly from Russia, Poland, Lithuania, and Hungary—were mass-deserting their Orthodox roots and their traditional synagogues. They flocked en masse into Reform Jewish synagogues, which up to this period had been strictly ethnic bastions for German Jews.

To be brutally honest, it was a German ethnicity that snobbishly and deliberately shied away from any religious and social contact with non-German Jews. My own congregation in West Hartford is a classic example. It was originally founded by German Orthodox Jews in 1843. During the 1870s, the congregation switched its religious practice and affiliation to the burgeoning Reform movement in the United States. The congregation, however, remained a tight German-Jewish enclave until just before World War II with a membership of about 250 German-Jewish families. During the two decades following the war, over a thousand new Greater Hartford families joined the congregation. Nine out of ten of these new members came to German Reform Judaism from East European Orthodox Jewish backgrounds, and many from Conservative Jewish congregations. Today, out of a membership of fourteen hundred families, barely 5 percent are of German-Jewish descent.

Ironically, had it not been for the mass postwar infusion of Eastern European Jews from Orthodox and Conservative backgrounds into the Reform movement, American Reform Judaism would not today be the largest Jewish denomination. A further irony is that the prewar German-Jewish Reform congregations would not have been around to absorb the huge wave of East European Jews clamoring for Reform affiliation because their original German-Jewish constituency was rapidly dying out by the late 1930s, with few German Jews left to replace their elders.

While the East Europeans brought with them into their new Reform affiliation many unpleasant memories and mixed religious emotions pertaining to their Orthodox upbringing which they were anxious to be rid of, their happy memories of the Bar Mitzvah ritual for their sons remained an emotionally and religiously warm and positive memory. Reform's new members had no objection whatsoever to having their sons and daughters confirmed together at age sixteen or to the extended coeducational high school in Judaism that accompanied the Confirmation rite. But many of the newcomers pressured their rabbis and the boards of their temples to offer the Bar Mitzvah rite to new members who opted for the thirteen-year-old male ritual.

Within a short time, the overwhelming majority of Reform congregations had reintroduced the Bar Mitzvah ritual, although many Reform rabbis were apprehensive. Their main concern was that the thirteen-year-old boys would drop out of their Jewish studies immediately following the Bar Mitzvah and choose not to go on to Confirmation three years later. In time, sadly, this is exactly what transpired. By the late 1990s, the Bar Mitzvah dropout rate in the average Reform congregation had become a national Jewish educational disaster, with close to 50 percent of the youngsters now terminating their Jewish studies directly following the Bar Mitzvah.

What was even more pathetic is that young Jewish women began to drop out as well at age thirteen. In the postwar decades, Reform congregations added the female ritual of Bat Mitzvah to their life-cycle ceremonies, whereby girls could now enjoy the same coming-of-age religious experience as boys. The downside, affecting both Reform Judaism and even the Conservative movement, however, is that while Bar and Bat Mitzvah is now the life-cycle rage, Jewish student congregational ranks are plummeting in the post-thirteen-year-old age groups, and today only skeletal numbers remain for Confirmation and continuing serious pre-college Jewish education.

Bad enough to suffer a curriculum of religious education which is short-circuited in early adolescence, creating a generation of Jewish illiterates! Worse yet, the social and culinary fanfare that often accompanies modern-day Bar/Bat Mitzvah celebrations makes an even greater mockery of Judaism. Jewish caterers vie with each other to arrange the "mother of all" buffets and carnival banquets of pagan-gorging proportions. The simple schnapps and kichel and herring post-service receptions of the past have given way to Cecil B. DeMille–like banquet hall and country-club settings featuring a sea of gourmet food stations that hawk both kosher and trefe delicacies from the far corners of the globe. A new generation of lavish Jewish party planners has emerged inventively at work "out-theme-ing" each other with dazzling disco circuses of pubescent delights that keep hordes of partying thirteen-year-olds stomping through the night in their weekly cycle of Bar/Bat Mitzvah fun and games.

I'm all for rejoicing in this age group entering Jewish young adulthood. But Jewish young adulthood historically carried with it a sacred responsibility and serious public commitment to utilize the teenage years to broaden and deepen one's intellectual and spiritual ties to Judaism. Age thirteen was but the first significant step on what was considered to be a lifetime Jewish journey and obligation.

In the past fifty or sixty years, far too many American Jewish parents have taken total leave of their educational and religious senses and shamefully allowed, if not encouraged, their children, after Bar/Bat Mitzvah, to abandon their Jewish education at the very moment in their young lives when they need it most. What has pathetically ensued is not only a thirteen- to eighteen-year-old age gap in Jewish intellectual and religious experience; but this vast Jewish wasteland is generally extended through the college years and beyond, so that young Jewish men and women have today become indifferent strangers and shameful bystanders to their heritage. Growing to maturity in a complete Jewish vacuum of this sort, is it any wonder then when interfaith dating occurs, the Jewish partner is totally unprepared to cope with the problems and challenges of Jewish-Christian relations and the religious responsibilities in a mixed marriage, especially where there is no conversion to each other's faith, or even in an intermarriage where conversion of the non-Jew to Judaism does takes place.

In my forty-three years of pre-marriage counseling of interfaith couples, I encountered so many non-Jewish women who, in the privacy of my study, openly scorned their Jewish partners for their total indifference if not alienation toward their Jewish roots and upbringing—whose push for the conversion of the non-Jew was generally motivated exclusively by a hysterical parent or grandparent who could not abide the prospect of their child marrying someone not "of the faith."

10

Establishing Jewish Identity
for Children of Mixed Marriages

Contrary to what many people believe, Jews included, Jewish descent is not established solely through the mother, or what is known as matrilineal descent. Not too many modern-day Jews realize that in biblical and rabbinical law, Jewish descent was through the father—patrilineal descent. At the same time, Jewish law also declared that when a marriage was not a legally accepted marriage, the child of such a marriage followed the status of the mother.

In time, however, descent only through the mother became the norm in Jewish life and law because, while the paternity of a child could oftentimes be challenged and questioned, the maternity of the child was far more certain. In our generation, the Orthodox and Conservative movements both maintain that *only* matrilineal descent determines who is Jewish from birth. Thus, in a marriage between a Jewish father and a non-Jewish mother, the child, in traditional Judaism, automatically follows the non-Jewish mother's religion irrespective of the father's religion. If, however, a non-Jewish mother chooses to convert to Orthodoxy or Conservatism, then her child becomes fully Jewish through her conversion, although both of these branches of Judaism require that the child be converted as well.

Reform Judaism, up to 1983, also followed establishing Jewish descent through the mother. Reform, however, was never truly comfortable with the idea of accepting *biology* as the sole criterion for establishing or guaranteeing Jewish descent. Reform was far more open and accepting of establishing one's Jewish "credentials" through the vehicle of conviction and not conception. In Reform Judaism's viewpoint, one is not really "born" to the faith. Reform contends that one is bred into the faith—through years of learning, practice, role-modeling, and true devotion. What additionally has led the Reform movement into ranking patrilineal descent on the same level as matrilineal descent is the Reform movement's caring, daring, and emergency response to the tidal wave of intermarriages sweeping the American Jewish community during the last half of the twentieth century.

When I was first ordained in 1951, barely one in five Jewish marriages was an intermarriage. By the early 1980s, nearly half of Jewish marriages in this country were between Jews and non-Jew. In the vast majority of these intermarriages, the husbands were Jewish. Even now, almost fifty years later, Jewish men predominate in seeking non-Jewish wives. What is also still prevalent is that the largest number of gentile women are still coming into Judaism from Catholic backgrounds, with a significantly smaller number turning away from Protestant upbringing. Happily, waves of these intermarried couples have been genuinely anxious to become a full-fledged part of the Jewish community. Interfaith counseling has revealed that the majority of the intermarried couples also fervently wish to affiliate with the synagogue and raise their children Jewishly.

In May of 1983, the Central Conference of American Rabbis, responding to this dramatic surge of mixed marriages (i.e., marriages between a Jew and an *un*converted non-Jew) and taking advantage of the new and bracing spirit of egalitarianism in our present generation, went on record with the following resolution:

> The CCAR declares that the child of one Jewish parent is under the presumption of Jewish descent. This presumption

of the Jewish status of the offspring of any mixed-marriage through the Jewish Father, however, is to be clearly established through appropriate and timely public and formal acts of identification with the Jewish faith.

Where the non-Jewish mother chooses not to convert through this 1983 resolution, the presumption of Jewish descent is then clearly established through the Jewish father, as such descent was once established in ancient times. But with one major caveat! What must be clearly and maturely understood is that this "presumption" of Jewish descent must be firmed up and followed up by the couple's sincere declaration that they *both* want to live Jewish lives together; and that they both agree to raise their children Jewishly. Further, this "presumption of Jewish descent" requires that the couple immediately begin to involve themselves in "appropriate and timely public and formal acts of identification with the Jewish faith and people." These very specific acts leading toward a positive and exclusive Jewish identity are clearly understood to include entry into the Covenant by way of circumcision (berit), the acquisition of a Hebrew name, regular attendance at religious school, Bar/Bat Mitzvah, and Confirmation. For those beyond childhood claiming Jewish identity, other inspired public acts or declarations may be added or substituted after consultation with their congregational rabbi.

All of the above, it is vital to note, is in full keeping with Reform Judaism's historical contention that meaningful Jewish religious status ideally hinges, not upon blood and genetics alone, but is equally dependent upon daily and lifetime acts of Jewish commitment, practice, loyalty, and devotion. The upside to the Reform Jewish ruling on patrilineal descent is that it has enabled many thousands of mixed-married couples to affiliate with Reform synagogues. And it has mandated the average Reform synagogue to reach out warmly and energetically to these interfaith couples to make them fully aware that they are indeed welcome. The major downside to Reform's patrilineal ruling is the bitter opposition to this ruling from Orthodox and Conservative Jewish quarters. They claim that the patrilineal ruling will further separate and fracture the larger Jewish community, not only in prime matters of birth, but in matters of basic Jewish identity, conversion, marriage, and divorce.

The expected traditionalist Jewish breast-beating and sectarian name-calling, however, has had little or no impact upon Reform rabbis and laypersons. The Reform Jewish resolve in this matter has firmed up even more strongly with the mass Reform effort to deal with the ever-growing phenomenon of intermarriage. The less rigid among Conservative Jewry, whether clergy or laypersons, are slowly beginning to rouse themselves to this same outreach challenge. Within this coming generation, Conservative Judaism will, I believe, follow Reform's lead and mount a parallel and vigorous outreach effort.

One other downside of the patrilineal issue disturbingly confronts the Reform movement. What many Reform rabbis and lay leaders are witnessing is the not-to-be-dismissed reality of far too many ignorant and even deceitful Jewish males who are elated with the knowledge that the children of their non-Jewish wives can now be considered legitimately Jewish according to Reform's new patrilineal ruling. However, many of these same Jewish husbands and fathers are conveniently overlooking their larger Jewish responsibilities in this same patrilineal ruling to see to it that their children's Jewish identity is immediately and fully established through ongoing appropriate and timely public and formal acts of identification with Judaism, such as Bris, baby naming, Sunday school, Bar/Bat Mitzvah, and Confirmation. In the last decade of my own rabbinical career, I still vividly remember the many calls I took in my study from nervous and excitable Jewish men who wanted me to confirm instantly over the phone the fact that Reform Judaism would now consider their children fully

Jewish even though their fiancées were not Jewish. "Isn't *that*, Rabbi, what the patrilineal ruling is all about?" I would immediately respond: "You're only half-way there, my friend, if you think that *your* Jewish descent alone will automatically cover your kids! Read the *whole* resolution again! You obviously have not bothered to understand that unless you, as a Jew, are genuinely willing and totally prepared to commit yourself now to be the best Jew possible for your future children, not to mention your gentile wife, don't kid yourself into believing that your Jewish responsibilities begin and end with the mere presumption of Jewish descent!"

I am not declaring that this simple-minded male Jewish approach to patrilineal descent represents a major new wrinkle for Reform Judaism to worry itself about or even consider the revoking of the 1983 patrilineal ruling. However, Reform Judaism does have a formidable problem and challenge out there at the moment to remind all those caught up in this wave of intermarriage frenzy that the historically gnawing question of "who really is a Jew?" has no simplistic and uncomplicated answer.

11

Speaking Good or Ill
About the Dead
(or, Doing Justice to the Deceased)

The most emotionally demanding responsibility in my profession is the funeral. Shepherding the different generations of a grieving family through the cycle of dying, death, and mourning was always unsettling. Despite the fact that legions of families gratifyingly extolled my eulogies for their loved ones, as well as my professional and personal ministrations extended to the family sorrowfully caught up in the experience of expected or even totally unexpected death, a call from someone in the family or the mortician apprising me of a death never failed to trigger in me a reaction of deep unease and inadequacy. One would think that as the years went by in my profession, a clergyman would get reasonably used to officiating at this highly stressful type of life-cycle event. Many do. But I was never one of them.

A great part of my rabbinical unease at funerals centered around my deep personal awareness of the general inadequacy of words of eulogy to meaningfully and accurately characterize the life and the impact of the deceased. Even when a rabbi has been particularly close to a congregant, both in temple life as well as in one's personal life, while there is invariably much to praise about the deceased, there still remained multi-tiered levels of deeper impact, achievement, and bless-

ing which only a spouse, a son or daughter, a parent, a grand-
child, a sibling, a really close friend, or a life-time co-worker
could fittingly give voice to. Whenever I met with the bereaved
family to prepare for a funeral service, I always encouraged
family members and really close associates of the deceased to
add, if they chose to do so, their own indispensable words of
personal eulogy at the funeral service. My only caveat to those
who volunteered to speak was to have them write out their
eulogies in advance. Then, if they understandably faltered or
froze while speaking at the funeral service, which oftentimes
has awkwardly happened, I could step in and finish their text
for them.

The first hurdle to overcome upon my learning about a
death was to make a decision as to where to meet with the family to prepare for the funeral service—in the privacy of my
study, in the deceased's home, or at the funeral chapel. Since
the family generally had to go to the mortuary first to discuss
the emotionally unsettling logistics and mind-popping financial costs surrounding death and burial, and since the funeral
parlor was just several blocks away from my temple, I generally arranged to meet with the family there. In more cases than
not, however, my own study or the home of the deceased was
an emotionally easier setting for the rabbi-family meeting.

In the two Jewish communities I served in my career,
Pittsburgh and Hartford, I always had two bones of contention
with local funeral directors. One was to convince the family
that they did not have to formally receive condolence-callers in
the mortuary chapel directly before the funeral service, which
was a long-standing custom in Pittsburgh, even to the point
where the funeral director routinely arranged to have the family receive mourners the evening before the funeral, as well as
an hour before the service began in the funeral chapel. Jewish
law and custom, few modern Jews realize, actually prohibits
this type of *pre*-funeral visitation, whether at home or at the
mortuary, so that the family can be assured of complete priva-

cy and sufficient comfort time before the funeral. After the interment in the cemetery, Jewish practice sensitively dictates, is the *sole* appropriate time for visitation.

This pre-funeral "calling" custom continually upset me. Where I could, I strongly urged families to resist bowing to this micro-managing by many funeral directors. Having to endure a formal receiving-line visitation, as in Pittsburgh the night before the funeral, invariably boiled down to a cocktail-party atmosphere without the drinking and having to endure raucous conversations centering around inane party chit-chatting. Even having to endure receiving-line visitation directly before the funeral service oftentimes imposed an unnecessarily harsh emotional and physical burden upon the bereaved family, who just wanted to be left alone in their initial period of private sorrow while girding themselves for the emotional ordeal of the funeral service and the mass visitation to follow.

My second bone of contention with funeral directors, and this was mainly in the last community I served for a quarter of a century, was my own strong personal and professional preference for funeral services to be held only in the temple. The funeral directors generally encouraged the family to use their chapels at the mortuary rather than have the service at the synagogue. Most of my members were unaware that the congregational by-laws of our historic congregation allowed every single member the right and privilege of a *temple* funeral. In far too many Jewish congregations in America, traditional and liberal, the right of temple burial is reserved for the top lay leadership of the institution or for members considered "machers" (VIP's) in the community. Even members who were aware that the temple setting was an option for burial were oftentimes intimidated by the majestic size of our main sanctuary. They feared that mourners attending the service might be embarrassingly lost amid the vast sea of empty pews. Our congregation, however, also offered a beautiful small chapel which was generally perceived to be too small for the average-sized funeral attendance. The mortuary hall down the street generally appeared to be a more comfortable physical fit for the average funeral attendance. For me, however, there was never any question that the temple sanctuary alone was the ideal emotional and spiritual setting for *any* grieving family and guests. Even if the deceased and the family were no more than High Holy Day worshippers at best, the synagogue, majestic or modest-sized, I believed, offered the most comforting and the most spirit-lifting religious ambience for their grief and their hopes. In wrestling with this option, family upon family over the years thanked me profusely for helping them to decide upon having the funeral in the temple.

Once the decision regarding place had been made, a larger tension oftentimes loomed between rabbi and grieving family, particularly in situations where the deceased's lifetime relations with the spouse and with children, grandchildren, and siblings had been less than perfect. One pre-funeral session I had years and years ago still haunts me. I was meeting with the widow and four of the deceased's grown children. From their combined outer appearance of non-grieving and almost sullen facial expressions and squirmingly restless body language, I quickly sensed that I was going to have great difficulty not only in getting them to talk about the deceased but to really level with me as to the essential character and spirit of the deceased which I needed to create even the simplest of eulogies. What few halting words of remembrance the widow was able to contribute in the face of my gentle but insistent urging came out with painful difficulty. I had no personal knowledge of her husband, nor did I really know the wife and the four children either. As she spoke, the widow furtively looked to each of her sullen children for support, confirmation, and pleading understanding.

The same difficulty seemed to grab hold of three of the four adult children. With great effort each of them seemed to be digging painfully deep for the tiniest nugget of praise surrounding their father's life and personality. When I finally turned to the last son and asked him pointedly if there was anything he might like to contribute to the family memory pool, he glowered at his siblings, and after a few seconds of embarrassed silence, he finally exploded, "Rabbi, my father was a total bastard!" The widow at that point broke down into violent sobbing and her other children ran over to her to console her. Once things quieted down, I turned to the openly embittered son and reminded him somewhat snidely that it was not in the tradition of Jewish eulogizing to include vituperative condemnation, even if his father were, in truth, the son-of-a-bitch he claimed. I was not contesting that. I, as the rabbi, just desperately needed something of even sparse public comment about the deceased that I might hang my brief eulogy upon. Like many of my colleagues in similarly shocking family situations, I was from time to time impelled to forsake even the faintest of tributes, scrapping the personal eulogy in favor of some general meditation about death or some fitting biblical psalm or even a comforting piece of poetry.

The distressing pre-funeral session with this family was thankfully not the norm in my career. But even in the majority of family situations, where many members were panting to let me know that they truly loved the deceased and genuinely wanted me to extol him or her to the skies, I must still confess that it was a never-ending challenge to deliver any eulogy because of the nagging doubt in my mind that I could never ever possibly do full justice to the deceased.

A funeral challenge of a totally different but equally sticky kind pertained to the occasional struggle to deal with the life of someone whom both the surviving family and the whole community knew was a complete mamser (i.e., bandit) who throughout life brought nothing but shame and humiliation to the family as well as to the world at large. Having to officiate at the funerals of such blackguards was indeed the supreme test of language, restraint, and ingenuity. But whether black-

guard or saint, facing any throng of mourners generally produced in me nothing but inner queasiness and inadequacy.
What particularly unsettled me—and all of my colleagues as
well, I'm sure—was the continuing knowledge that at the
funeral the clergyman is always listened to with more rapt personal attention than at any other life-cycle moment. Even when
I tried to distance myself from the life of a departed saint or
sinner by publicly declaring that "it was not my privilege or
pleasure to know the deceased personally," and even though I
generally relied only on intimates of the deceased for totally
honest value judgments, whatever I managed to highlight in
my eulogy, I still sensed it left much to be desired for the rank-
and-file mourners before me.

12

Ecumenical Squirming and the Unbridgeable Divide in Interfaith Dialogue

In the early years of my ministry in Pittsburgh, particularly during the thirteen exciting years between 1955 and 1968 when I was rabbi of Pittsburgh's first suburban Reform Jewish congregation in the township of Mount Lebanon, interfaith outreach dominated my rabbinate. No Reform temple had heretofore existed in Pittsburgh's sprawling South Hills suburbs, and I was well aware that I would be called upon to relate professionally and personally to a vast spectrum of Christian life which had heretofore little or no contact with the Jewish community.

Unlike other major cities in America, which after World War II recorded a tremendous shift of Jewish population from the inner city to the suburbs, Pittsburgh's inner-city Jewish population, which resided basically in an aging area of the city known as Squirrel Hill, strangely bucked the suburban move. By the early 1950s over 90 percent of Pittsburgh's Jewish community still stubbornly remained in place. Even half a century later, with the turn of the millennium, despite the significant growth of my former suburban temple in Mount Lebanon, as well as the presence of a Conservative congregation located in adjacent Scott Township, 80 percent of Pittsburgh's larger Jewish community still remains rooted in the Squirrel Hill section of the city. This virtual self-ghettoization puzzled and irked me greatly during my seventeen-year Pittsburgh rabbinate, where for the first four years of my career I ministered in the city as assistant rabbi at the historic Rodef Shalom congregation. I was originally of the opinion that the Pittsburgh suburbs would attract a substantial portion of the larger Jewish community. The suburban schools, particularly in Mount Lebanon, were among the best in the country. Real estate was ample and invitingly inexpensive for young families. Suburban access to downtown Pittsburgh offices, shopping, culture, and sports was a breeze compared to other major metropolitan areas in the country. In trying to figure out the long-standing insularity of the Squirrel Hill Jewish community, I finally had to chalk it up to a hypersensitively parochial Jewish provincialism that would never substantially change.

While the thirteen years I led the suburban temple in Mount Lebanon were rich with exciting and highly rewarding congregational and personal growth and fulfillment, I still despaired that the congregation there and the suburban Jewish community at large would never reach its full and natural Jewish potential.

Quite frankly, when the call from my next pulpit came to me in the winter of 1967, I accepted because I sensed that the South Hills Pittsburgh Jewish community had reached a plateau of growth where it would in time expand no further. Had Pittsburgh's urban Jewry shifted a significant part of its constituency from the city to its suburbs while I was serving there, I would probably never have left Pittsburgh and, with relish and fulfillment, would have remained there for the next thirty-two years of my career. For me, personally, it was not the typical "bigger is better" clergy syndrome that impelled me to leave Pennsylvania and spend the major concluding part of my career in Connecticut. I just fantasized that a somewhat larger chunk of Pittsburgh Jewry would focus a more proportionate share of its unique and historical community size, strength, and diversity into a challengingly new and vital area of the city that could benefit from a larger Jewish presence. But it was not meant to be.

If I missed dealing with a larger number of Jews in my Pittsburgh suburban ministry, there was absolutely no shortage of non-Jews. Even though my congregation, Temple Emanuel, excitingly grew within a decade from 150 families to almost 600, with a religious school of 500 children, our temple was still a tiny oasis of Jewish life set against the huge landscape of Protestant and Catholic suburban churches. Since it took a while for my temple to build its majestic modern-style sanctuary to house its members fully for High Holiday worship and other state occasions, in the early years of our congregational history I was forced to seek out neighboring churches and public schools to temporarily accommodate our members. In our pre–main sanctuary era, our congregation was warmly and graciously welcomed to pray in a whole series of neighboring Presbyterian, Baptist, Congregational, and Methodist churches. During our protracted building era, our religious school met for over a year in a neighboring Roman Catholic church. During that same period, the congregation conducted its regular Sabbath evening and morning worship in the interdenominational chapel on the grounds of a nearby county hospital.

My having to contact so many Christian clergy for the periodic use of their churches happily paved the way for a wealth of interfaith personal and professional contacts that set the pattern for years of breakthrough and truly significant and meaningful ecumenical Christian-Jewish dialogue, pulpit exchanges, and mass intercongregational educational and social programming. Early on in this intensive ambassadorial outreach period of my suburban rabbinate, I made a vital career ecumenical decision which, unfortunately, was not the norm among many of my rabbinical colleagues at the time— and even today.

On the one hand, in my constant explaining of Judaism to Christians, I naturally wanted non-Jews to be cognizant of the many, many similarities between our faiths. That is to say, we all worship the same God. We all seek authority from the same sacred books of the Old Testament. And, by and large, Jews and Christians all accept the moral imperatives of Mosaic law. But for rabbis to achieve a totally sincere and truly honest sense of brotherhood, I went out of my way to declare and demand that both Jew and Christian should never for one moment gloss over or minimize the vast and profound religious differences and the gaping religious divide that has always separated our two great faiths—and always will, I still believe, even with the best and most strenuous of our interfaith efforts and intentions.

My life-time preaching and teaching ecumenical mission has always mandated me as a rabbi to confront this classic divide head-on and impel every non-Jew listening to me to come to maturely understand, appreciate, and respect the vast religious differences between us. Sadly, far too many of my Jewish colleagues, and my Christian colleagues as well, have missed the ecumenical boat by proceeding to paper over or completely water down the deep, profound, and complex interreligious "divide" that has always existed, and, frankly, will always exist, between our religions.

Over all the years of my rabbinate, even if I have made both Jews and non-Jews initially squirm, I have made an ecumenical career of beginning and winding up all of my interfaith preaching and teaching by declaring, "I do not want your tolerance! I do not want any of us, Jew or Gentile, to patronize or misunderstand one other. I simply want us to come to realize that the Old Testament world you share with me and I share with you has some startlingly different, divisive, and ultimately irreconcilable spiritual and moral mandates, values, and challenges. And, since that is so, our priority goal in down-to-earth interfaith dialogue must be nothing less than to can-

didly but respectfully face up to this divide and go on realistically and honestly from there!"

Where the Jewish and Christian worlds collide most
sharply is first and foremost in Judaism's ringing answer to the
age-old doctrinal question, "Are people born basically good or
bad?"

Catholics and Conservative Protestants have been weaned
upon St. Paul's nineteen-hundred-year-old doctrine of original sin. This is that paramount and classic teaching of the
church which proclaims that *everyone* born into this world is
born with some taint of the same sin that attached itself to
Adam when he committed the original sin by disobeying
God's command in Genesis forbidding him to eat from the tree
of good and evil. That *original* sin, according to Paul and the
early Church fathers, resulted in man's falling away from
God's grace. Christians, however, are taught that they can be
fully restored to divine grace by doing three essential things.
First, by being baptized at birth in the name of the Father, the
Son, and the Holy Spirit. Such Baptism helps to wash away the
stain of Adam's grievous sin. Second, by performing good ethical works throughout their lives. And third, by believing in
Christ as the messianic Son of God who was sent by God to
redeem all mankind from sin and usher in the messianic age.
However, it is *only* through believing in Jesus, according to
Christianity, that a person can be saved—saved in the belief
that through Jesus' death upon the cross, human beings take
all of human sin and suffering upon their own shoulders, thus
paving the way for life everlasting with Christ and God.

Many non-Jews are astonished when they learn that in
Judaism neither the central figure of Jesus nor the Christian
idea of salvation plays any role whatsoever in human behavior
or in the radically different Jewish understanding of the basic
nature of man. For Jews, traditional and liberal, all of the early
tales in Genesis, preceding the appearance of the patriarch
Abraham, are treasured mainly for their grand poetic and leg-

endary Aesop-like moral import. The stories of Adam and Eve, Cain and Abel, Noah's Ark, and the Tower of Babel were never looked upon by the Jewish biblical writers and later generations of rabbinical commentators as basic religious building blocks for understanding human nature. The charming and timeless Genesis stories have been treasured over the ages for their ethical and human challenges and insights. From the Jewish perspective, *all* men and women are envisioned as being born not inherently *bad* but innately *good*. The Talmud of old set the majestic tone for the natural, inborn goodness with a moving morning prayer that is found in the daily Orthodox Jewish prayer book, "My God, the soul which Thou gavest unto me is pure!"

Our sages, however, were quick to stress that while people are all born *inherently* good, mankind is also born with a parallel powerful predisposition toward evil. Long before Sigmund Freud, Judaism keenly and frankly understood that our human capacity for evil was not only born with us, but that over our lifetime the evil impulses in our basic nature can become even stronger than our good impulses. The rabbis referred to the good impulse as the *yetser ha-tov* and the evil impulse as the *yetser ha-ra*. Our fathers saw the classic battle between good and evil within us human beings as constituting a fierce and never-ending struggle from the womb to the tomb. In Judaism, a good person is defined as any man or woman who learns how to control the evil impulses within and fully allows the good impulses to assert themselves front and center at every stage of life.

Where the key doctrinal issue of salvation enters into the Jewish ethical scenario is in the long-accepted Jewish contention that upon death God will ultimately make the final judgment upon every human life. And that final judgment is to be based *exclusively* upon our own individual human success in accomplishing what amounts to a lifelong balancing act between the good and evil drives within our personalities.

Putting it more directly, if ultimately the moral balance in our lives is not heavily tipped in favor of the good, we mortals will inevitably jeopardize our craved-for eternity with God. That is to say, every single Jew is taught by Judaism that all that can essentially "save' us or "redeem" us in the larger ethical scheme of things is our own God-given inborn mortal capacity to live the moral life. No Hebrew prophet put it more powerfully than Micah (6:8): "The Lord has told us what is good. What God requires of us is to do what is just, to demonstrate unending love, and to live in humility with both God and man."

Spelling it out even more, our living what is normally referred to as the holy life, from the classic Jewish perspective, is even more simply characterized and sharply defined in Leviticus 19. Holiness, in Judaism, fundamentally consists chiefly of providing for the poor, refraining from stealing, cheating, or lying, being honest and just when making daily decisions in legal matters, not bearing a grudge unduly, and loving your neighbor as you love yourself. Sinning, in Judaism, is thus basically conceived of as shamefully separating ourselves from God and from other people.

What many Christians are further shocked to learn about the Jewish ethic, as contrasted with the Christian ethic, is that Judaism has always been conceived as a "do it yourself" kind of ethic wherein a Jesus figure plays no role whatsoever. What the average Christian has found terribly difficult to accept is that the Jews, in a word, have never and will never look to any "Jesus-like" savior for their ultimate salvation. In Judaism, built into our basic nature, endowed by God alone, are to be found all of the ethical and spiritual tools we will ever need to shape up morally and spiritually in an attempt to do full, ongoing justice to our divine potential. Over the years of my interfaith speaking, whenever I proceeded to explain this paramount aspect of Judaism, I always sensed in my heart and mind that it would probably seem inconceivable if not impossible for the average Christian to believe that there actually exist blood relatives of Jesus who live their entire lives and face eternity without Jesus being totally pivotal to their existence.

A second major and equally sharp divide that further separates Christian from Jew, and will, I believe, continue to separate and estrange them, deals with the equally intriguing doctrine of the coming of the Messiah. What basically differentiates the early Hebrew prophetic ideas about the Messiah from New Testament messianic thinking is that the Hebrew prophets in the Old Testament never believed in the coming of an actual Messiah, redeemer, or deliverer. Theirs was rather the passionate age-old Jewish conviction that a better *time* was coming—a messianic age not only for Jews but for *all* mankind! It was not until later, in the period of savage Roman oppression of the Jews in ancient Palestine two thousand years ago, that there gradually emerged the bold poetic idea of the coming of a messianic *person* who was to be designated by God to usher in the messianic era. Since the early history of the Jews in Palestine was bound up gloriously and inseparably with the ancient Hebrew monarchy, it was only natural that such a messianic person would be imagined in a regal form. And, since the one great king in all of Israel's ancient history was the beloved King David, it was only natural that as the Hebrew masses began to long for the coming of a messianic redeemer and savior from Roman oppression, such a messianic figure would be an idealized King David. It was during this oppressive Roman period that a special prayer for the coming of the Messiah was inserted by the ancient rabbis into the daily prayer ritual of our forefathers. To this very day, traditional Jews recite the following daily messianic prayer: "Speedily cause the offspring of David, thy servant, to flourish, and lift up his glory by Thy divine help, because we wait for Thy salvation all the day. Blessed art Thou, O Lord, Who causes the strength of messianic hope and salvation to flourish."

When the Reform movement developed at the beginning of the nineteenth century, its founding fathers rejected the belief in the coming of a *personal* Messiah. Reform Judaism harked back to the Hebrew prophets and their original plea and hope for the coming of a morally improved *society*. Reform Judaism also uniquely stressed the personal responsibility of the individual to help bring about this messianic time. In other words, in the Jewish historical perspective, as clearly differentiated from the Christian messianic concept, the coming of a messianic person or a messianic age hinges exclusively, not upon *God's* intervention, as in Christian doctrine through the person of Jesus, but upon our own ongoing *individual* willingness and personal passion to stand in the forefront of human progress and societal change.

Christians are often quite shaken to learn that in Judaism the Messiah's coming is strictly contingent not upon the coming or second coming of Jesus, but upon each and every generation doing what is morally urgent to repair this very imperfect world! *Every* man and woman, Judaism declares, has the divine capacity and built-in human potential to become a practical and inspired personal herald for the coming of the messianic age.

Still another mystifying divide between Christians and Jews deals with the intriguing fact that there is scarcely a doctrinal trace of the ideas of heaven and hell, resurrection and immortality in the entire Jewish Bible! Despite countless Old Testament references and quotations found in the New Testament, dealing with any number of religious issues and personalities, it comes as a major jolt for the average Christian to learn that there was absolutely no specific Jewish doctrine dealing with the subject of a heavenly paradise or of a life after death until around the first century *before* Christianity, long after the Jewish Bible was completed.

I have always appreciated that it was very difficult for the average Christian religious audience to believe that there was never any Jewish speculation as to what follows death. Actually, there was! In ancient times, it was always centered upon the ultimate destiny of the Jewish nation and the Jewish state, but not upon the destiny of the individual. Before the Babylonian Exile in the sixth pre-Christian century, the prevailing theory about the hereafter was that upon death, the spirit or soul of the individual entered into a shadowy, vaguely defined underworld called *Sheol*. In early Jewish thinking. Sheol was imagined as an eerie, other-worldly place that received all of the dead. There was no judgment and no distinction between good people and bad. One was simply dead, and that was all there was to it! Life terminated in Sheol. There was no concept of a personal afterlife.

When the ancient Jewish nation was destroyed by the Babylonians in 586 B.C.E., and faith in the future *national* destiny of Israel was severely shaken, then and only then did the Jews begin to look inward and upward for some personal and theological way out of their religious and personal destiny. Under the influence of the prophet Ezekiel, around five hundred years *before* Christ, there slowly began to develop a vague belief in some sort of personal retribution in a life *after* death for each human being. This incipient personal afterlife, however, was always directly related to the moral quality of the life one lived in *this* world.

During the oppressive Roman period in Jewish history, Sheol became a sort of underground "waiting room" for the dead. The dead, that is to say, were conceived to remain in this suspended state until the Last Judgment. At that undefined future time, God would decide whether the individual was to receive eternal damnation or eternal bliss. Sheol subsequently became merged with another Hebrew term *Gehenna*, which was understood to be a strictly figurative equivalent of hell.

It was actually the rabbis of the first century, known as the Pharisees, who finally put some doctrinal flesh on the bones of this developing concept of heaven and hell. They formulated the doctrine, still accepted by the traditional Jews of today, that at death people fall into three basic categories—the completely righteous, the completely wicked, and the intermediate. After death the righteous person went immediately to heaven, and the wicked directly to hell. The Pharisees maintained that God usually bent over backwards in judging the "intermediate" group. Most of the people in this category ultimately went to heaven. As to who were supposed to be the ideal, sure-fire candidates for this vaguely defined heaven, a famous ancient rabbi, Akiva, put it candidly:

> Those who were charitable, buried the dead, visited the sick, dealt honestly in business, loaned money to those in need, cared for orphans, were peace-makers when the situation called for it, instructed the poor, studied the Law and were martyrs for the faith.

As to what this state of heaven would be like, mainstream Jewish thinking down through the centuries, unlike Christianity, deliberately steered away from imagining any detailed or colorful descriptions of life *after* death. Jewish sages over the centuries never permitted normative Judaism to drift in the Christian direction of envisioning either other-worldly, heavenly delights or fantasizing grimly about Dantesque hell-like horrors. Judaism essentially has only wanted to *spiritualize* the concept of paradise. The rabbis wanted to make it crystal-clear to all Jews that human beings were to serve God with absolutely *no* expectation of reward. Judaism therefore historically declared that it is the here-and-now, and not the here-after, that must dominate human thinking and living. Jews have been bidden to become "candidates for heaven," according to the practical ancient dictum of Rabbi Akiva.

In the last analysis, I am inspired to go along with what another great rabbi centuries ago declared even more Jewishly. When asked by his disciples as he was about to depart from this world about his innermost wish for paradise, this sage of old sighed expectantly: "I do not want Your Garden of Eden. I do not want Your world-to-come. I want only Thee, my God, Thee and Thee alone!"

In the final analysis, I have generally lost my Christian audiences most completely when I made them confront what I consider to be the *ultimate* divide between Judaism and Christianity: how Jews regard Jesus. Over the many, many years of interfaith dialogue, I have found that most non-Jews will respectfully listen to and even sensitively appreciate almost everything that I have outlined before, even though it may be worlds apart and completely alien to their own Christian upbringing. But when I go on to confront this most provocative issue of Jesus himself, and where Judaism believes Jesus fits into the scheme of things, that's when I know that I have really lost them.

That is to say, when I proceed to make a bottom-line distinction between the religion *of* Jesus, which I contend is Judaism, and the religion *about* Jesus, which I contend is Christianity, here the ultimate ecumenical "squirm" factor between Christians and Jews reaches its most troubling if not explosive peak. I, of course, have always profoundly realized that I am striking here at the very heart and core of Christian identity, flirting in their eyes with blasphemy, or at the least showing willful insensitivity.

Behind the age-old misunderstanding surrounding the image of Jesus in Christian-Jewish dialogue, the major sticking point is that the Christian Bible makes no bones about the historical fact that Jesus, in his generation, was a proud and committed Jew, not to mention his parents as well. All of Jesus' preaching and teaching, as set down movingly in the Gospel writings and elsewhere, reveal the inescapable fact that he preached and taught about the ancient ideals and aspirations of his Jewish forefathers as exemplified through the lives and ministries of countless generations of Hebrew prophets, rabbis, and sages.

What seems to be conveniently or deliberately ignored are Jesus' own dramatically explicit words in Matthew 15:24, "I was sent *only* to the lost sheep of Israel." And in John 4:22, Jesus proclaims even more emphatically that "salvation is from the *Jews*." Matthew makes it even more decisive when he has Jesus assert in chapter 5: "Think not that I have come to *abolish* them [the Jewish laws] but to fulfill them! For truly, I say to you, till heaven and earth pass away, not an iota, not a dot will pass from the Law until all is accomplished. "Whoever then relaxes one of the least of these commandments, so shall he be called least in the Kingdom of Heaven; but he who does them and teaches them shall be called great in the Kingdom of Heaven."

What many Christians also fail to accept is that no educated Jew has ever denied or shied away from that part of Christian teaching which has to do with the claim that Jesus was the long-awaited and heralded Messiah. The belief in a Messiah who was to come and redeem the Jews and all mankind from the cruel hand of oppression and persecution, as mentioned before, was already a very popular mass doctrine in the depressing and savage political atmosphere of Palestinian Jewry at and before the time of Christ. Jewish and Roman literary sources of that period reveal that scores of men in ancient Palestine made similar claims and were brutally crucified by the Romans for their messianic presumptions.

What is also terribly difficult for many Christians to accept in this connection, not knowing the historical background, is that factual historical references to Jesus are absolutely nonexistent in the Jewish and Roman sources of that time. The only Jesus source, all Bible scholars agree, is to be found in the New Testament, whose books were written a full generation or two *after* Jesus. In other words, we are not dealing here with eyewitness factual accounts of the crucifixion drama. The key issue is that even if Judaism were to deny the "historical" Jesus, which it never has, neither the Jewish masses of his time nor the Jewish religion down through the centuries has ever had any reason to reject Jesus the *man*, his life or his basic biblical teachings. Were we Jews to reject Jesus the Jew, as has been falsely claimed throughout history, we would, in effect, be rejecting everything that was eminently worthwhile in his life and teachings and in the teachings of the Jewish faith. What Jews "reject" is not, therefore, the religion *of* Jesus, but a great deal of the religion which grew up *about* Jesus long, long after his life—namely, the religion of *Christianity*, which was later developed by Paul and countless others about whom Jesus had no personal knowledge whatsoever.

Paul ultimately and radically departed from the ancient Jewish concept of the Messiah when he came to look upon Jesus not as a "flesh-and-blood" Messiah—which type of human Messiah the Jews were expecting—but as a mystical, supernatural figure of the kind that Paul saw in his dramatic vision on the road to Damascus. Paul moved even further away from the Jewish idea of the Messiah by actually identifying the figure of Jesus with God! Twice in his epistles, Paul even put Jesus *before* God (Thessalonians 2:16 and Ephesians 5:5). In essence, Paul preached "Jesus Christ as Lord" (II Corinthians 4:5). For us Jews, however, there has been and still is only the one, supreme, and unique source of divinity. We Jews accept no other.

There is one last unbridgeable divide between Christianity and Judaism which the average Christian, in my interfaith dialoguing experience, has always had the most trouble grappling with: Why do Jews have such great difficulty with the core Christian belief, as developed by Paul, that when Jesus died on the cross, his death made atonement for *all* of the sins of mankind? Paul maintained that it was for this very reason alone that God sent Jesus to earth in human form. His coming, that is to say, was to afford every single human being a direct personal avenue for forgiveness in Christ. I realize that it is almost impossible for the average Christian to accept the fact that the mother religion, Judaism, totally rejects the Christian idea that *any* human being can actually atone for the sins of *another* human being. Judaism maintains as well that the sinner, and the sinner alone, must by his or her own repentant moral behavior atone for individual sin and guilt. Judaism very simply declares that a Jesus figure cannot save us from earthly sin. Nor, for that matter, can even God alone save us! As I mentioned before, Judaism must be seen, first and foremost, as a "do-it-yourself" kind of salvation. People alone, in Jewish thinking, have the God-given inner power to save themselves by their own moral and ethical actions. It is not that we Jews could not use a little divine help now and again in trying to gain a closer and deeper communion with the Almighty. But when the theological chips are down, the Jewish religion allows for no divine or even quasi-divine intermediary between human beings and God. That kind of special help, our religion declares, must come primarily from within and not from without. As the psalmist declared, "God is nigh until all them that call upon Him, to all that call upon Him in truth" (Psalm 145:18).

Is it any wonder, then, that the average Christian feels completely estranged if not alienated from the acknowledged descendants of Jesus, who will never ever come to look upon Jesus as the supernatural mass-atoning and intermediating Christ? If one adds to this Judaism's flat rejection of so many other key church doctrines, such as original sin, the trinity, the Immaculate conception, and the virgin birth, is it really any wonder that even the most frank and far-reaching interfaith dialogue can never ever paper over these radically separate and divisive, if not totally contradictory, religious beliefs? The closest Judaism will ever come to acknowledging Jesus is to grant him an honored place in the inspired line of the ancient Hebrew prophets. In no way, however, even in this regard, does this imply that Jewish history looks upon Jesus in his generation as another Amos, Hosea, Micah, or Isaiah. From the

Jewish perspective, even as understood from the Gospel writings, what Jesus taught and preached in his generation had all of the familiar and noble hallmarks of Hebrew prophetic utterances going back centuries before Jesus lived. His moving parables and pronouncements in the New Testament inspiringly exemplify some of the best of this glorious prophetic tradition.

What probably rankles Christians most about the way Judaism views Jesus is that it has included him in the ranks of the rabbis of his time, known more familiarly to non-Jews as the Pharisees. Unfortunately, generations of Christians have understood the word "Pharisee," as used in the New Testament, as almost a dirty word. In Christian thought, the entire group of Pharisees has for centuries been invested, unfortunately and inaccurately, with strictly negative if not totally anti-Jewish connotations. Terms like "hypocrite" and "hard-line ideologue" come naturally to New Testament readers whenever the Pharisees are mentioned. In the Jewish tradition, however, the term "Pharisee" has always been highly regarded as a religious badge of honor! In the mainstream Jewish literary sources of that era, the Pharisees, in fact, were looked upon as being on the cutting edge of desperately needed Jewish reform and liberalization. The Christian tradition has blackened the reputation of the Pharisees as the "bad guys" of Jewish history. For Jews, however, the religious goal of the Pharisees, along with the Hebrew prophets of old, was strictly and proudly to humanize and edify every aspect of the ancient Mosaic legal tradition. Whatever anti-liberal Jewish religious forces there were in that era were not the Pharisees. They were, in fact, the priestly Sadducees, who were the hard-core fundamentalists of their time. The bold religious reforms that Jesus espoused, by and large, were cut from the same luminous cloth as those of the Pharisees. Therefore, another major part of the divide here relating to the "squirm factor" between Christians and Jews boils down to believing in Jesus primarily as a supreme God figure or acknowledging him strictly as a moral and ethical teacher and reforming preacher of the best and the most meaningful of prophetic and Pharisaic Judaism.

I realize that it is mighty tough to turn nineteen centuries of tragic Christian-Jewish misunderstanding on its head. Being a fervent optimist, however, the tragic twentieth century, for all of the anti-Semitic horrors heaped upon the Jewish people, has demonstrated at the turn of the millennium that all is not completely lost in attempting to develop a bold new, and long, long overdue, dramatic reappraisal of the historic Jewish-Christian divide. However, any significant breakthrough in all of these highly sensitive and deeply emotional areas in the face of nineteen hundred years of anti-Semitism and Christian-Jewish misunderstanding must daringly and creatively originate in every Catholic and Protestant seminary, pulpit and classroom. From there, alone, can bold new interfaith understanding and relationships perhaps emerge where the two utterly dissimilar and divisive religious worlds can come to coexist with each other more meaningfully, more respectfully, and more realistically.

13

What Makes the
State of Israel Jewish?
(or, What Really Defines Us Over There?)

In the early years of my rabbinate, on the messianic heels of the State of Israel's emergence in May of 1948, most Jews, outside of Israel and even within, had serious difficulty in ascribing any profound sense of Jewishness to the infant Jewish state. Once the Jewish population of the State of Israel became the overwhelming majority (today the Jewish quotient is more than 80 percent), many assumed that the mere presence of five million Jews in a six million overall Israeli population might well give the Jewish state a singular Jewishness. In the United States, by comparison, Jews constitute less than 2 percent of the total population. While American Jewry encompasses six million members, within the first decade of the twenty-first century the State of Israel will boast the single largest Jewish community in the world!

When I spoke to non-Jewish audiences over the years, they were generally stunned to learn that in the face of one billion Catholics, one billion Moslems, one billion Hindus, and about a quarter of a billion Protestants on this planet, the total world Jewish population today numbers no more than fourteen million. They were further shocked to learn that during World War II, one-third of the Jewish people were murdered by the

Nazis and their European collaborators—some six million Jewish men, women, and children!

Yet even in tallying up modern-day Israel's majority Jewish population, the numbers there are in no way indicative of Israel's essential Jewishness. I have always used the analogy between Israel and the United States in this connection. Israel, from its birth, was constituted first and foremost as a political democracy, and, as in its American big-brother democratic republic, no single religion among the total population at large has ever had special precedence, official recognition, or greater public standing over any other majority or minority religion. Thus, notwithstanding the vast majority of affiliated Protestants in America, not to mention another eighty million unaffiliated Christians, plus sixty million Catholics, America, by virtue of its Constitution, does not recognize any one single religion as the official religion of state. In the United States the Constitution declares a complete separation of church and state.

So, too, in Israel. Even though 80 percent of Israelis identify themselves as Jews, Judaism has never been and is not today the legally recognized religion of the state. What confuses many non-Jews, and many Jews as well, is the growing presence of a very small, tough, highly vocal minority of intensely Orthodox Jews who have never stopped clamoring for traditional Jewish law and customs to be officially recognized by Israel's parliamentary government as the law of the land. Since over 80 percent of Israeli Jews consider themselves to be in the camp of the almost totally secular, if not strongly un-Orthodox and even anti-Orthodox, Israel's alleged Jewishness obviously lies elsewhere in the modern Jewish state.

If the factors of majority Jewish population and Israel's democratic form of parliamentary government do not invest the Jewish state with anything resembling distinct Jewishness, is there, then, any other single factor in Israeli society today that could conceivably define Israel as uniquely Jewish? In my mind, the greatest single factor has always centered upon the inspired phenomenon of the State of Israel attempting to re-create a separate and full Jewish *civilization* in the Holy Land. Such a civilization encompasses the total complex of a people's language, land, culture, ethnicity, religion, law, ethics, and politics—as one speaks, for example, of French, English, German, or Russian civilization. I am specifically referring to the kind of civilization where a people independently and totally control their own society and their own history and shape their own destiny on the stage of world history. The truly unique phenomenon about Jewish history during these past nineteen hundred years is that the Jewish people have been remarkably able, throughout their long and tortured history, to sustain a separate and almost completely integrated Jewish civilization of their own, in and beyond their historic homeland, and in the face of overwhelmingly hostile external non-Jewish political forces that tightly controlled and totally dominated Jewish society.

In this connection, I have always tried to point out to those unfamiliar with Jewish history and world history that for a thousand years *before* Christianity there existed in ancient Judea (Palestine) a flourishing and full Jewish civilization and pervasive Jewish national identity. This millennium-long Jewish presence in the ancient Middle East was periodically beset by one great pagan world empire after another—Assyria, Babylonia, Persia, Greece, and Rome—each of which in succession attempted to overwhelm, control, and destroy it. Each ancient pagan world power, in turn, ultimately disappeared form the stage of world history; but the Jewish people and their unique culture and society have survived to this very day.

When Christendom succeeded the Roman Empire in the fourth century, the fifteen hundred years following witnessed a continuing and even greater fragmentation and disintegration of Jewish society. Christian Europe demonized and persecuted the tiny remnant of Jewry in its midst. To this very day it remains one of the great mysteries of history just how the European Jew was able to maintain and perpetuate any significant sense of cohesive Jewish group identity. Without question, the basic instrument of Jewish survival has always been Judaism's inspired and deathless grip upon the Jewish people. Jews were passionately determined that their loyalty to God, their steadfast practice of Mosaic law, and their unbreakable bond of Jewish peoplehood would enable them to preserve their own distinct culture and heritage. Jews dreamed and prayed that one day in the future, Jewish life and Jewish destiny would no longer be at the cruel and indifferent mercy of external, non-Jewish political powers. Since 1948, that ancient dream has been miraculously realized, at least for the one-third of world Jewry living in the reestablished State of Israel, no longer a messianic dream but a living, dynamic modern historic reality.

The first five decades of Jewish statehood, from 1948 to 2000, have witnessed the dramatic re-creation of a full Jewish society and civilization. On some levels, Israeli society is quite similar to many other modern civilizations. And yet, Israeli society is intriguingly different, as Israelis respond to their own unique historical heritage and to their own specific Jewish needs, moods, demands, and challenges. Twenty-two hundred years, of course, is a mind-boggling gap between the completely independent Maccabean Jewish civilization of the last Jewish state and today's twenty-first-century Israeli Jewish national society. However, if modern-day Israel, in its first half-century of reborn Jewish national life, is any indication of the Jewish people's passionate and relentless will to re-create another totally free and independent Jewish civilization in its ancient homeland, then the generations ahead seem bright with realistic hopes for substantive Jewish nationhood and Jewish fulfillment. Some overly harsh critics of modern political Zionism view the new Israeli society as ultimately becoming but another Levantine, Middle Eastern statelet with but the bare trappings of qualitative Jewish civilization. The dramatic facts on the ground of the Middle East, however, just in these first fifty years, bespeak a far more positive, exciting, and realizable Jewish reality.

Nation-building today, for Israel's more than six million Jews has focused not only upon the re-creation of a modern Jewish body politic, but on a body politic reconnected to the ancient Hebrew tongue, which has been made to leap from the Bible and prayer book to the realm of the university and the marketplace. Israel has become a vibrantly new-old culture both mundanely and sublimely Jewish. In the realm of the mundane, one encounters a blizzard of Hebrew street signs, Hebrew streetwalkers, Hebrew bus drivers, and Hebrew rock stars. In the realm of the sublime, one confronts, more significantly, a stunning network of Hebrew universities, publishing houses, symphony halls, and medical centers, all dipping into the cultural riches of over three millennia of the Jewish past. Perhaps the most sublime and thrilling feature of the modern State of Israel is its humanitarian open-door immigration policy. This has allowed instant Jewish citizenship for endangered fellow Jews seeking immediate sanctuary, hope, and freedom in a still-menacing world where, even though the horror of Nazism is dead, anti-Semitism is still darkly alive.

A half a century, admittedly, is far too short a span of time to determine whether a modern-style Jewry, totally controlling its own national and cultural destiny in its own historic homeland, can produce still another distinct entity and identity on the scale of its ancestral roots and accomplishments. The jury will have to remain out on that for at least several generations to come before the final verdict is in. As for the immediate challenging puzzler, What makes the Jewish state Jewish?, while cultural forces normally provide the clues for categorizing societies, frankly, there is no norm when it comes to under-standing the Jews in history and to defining Jewishness. Ever since Abraham of old, we Jews have defied the norm. Somewhere between the norm and the abnormal lies the ulti-mate answer. In the meanwhile, history has provided Israeli Jewry and world Jewry with a breathtaking opportunity not merely to define our destiny but to live and dramatically reshape it.

14

You're Kidding About Turning the Other Cheek, Aren't You?
(or, Old Testament Morality vs. New Testament Morality: Which Is More Realistic?)

While Judaism and Christianity have many things in common, in my lifelong lecturing and preaching to Christian audiences, I have never flinched from highlighting the basic differences. It has always been my deepest interfaith resolve, in addressing non-Jewish groups, never to paper over the fundamentally different religious insights and doctrines of Judaism and Christianity. What I have striven to achieve in interreligious dialogue is not to challenge the average non-Jew to agree with me, which would be both impossible and potentially insulting, but simply to respect the differences between us, as contradictory and disturbing as they may be. The differences are never, in my mind, to be looked upon as superior versus inferior, as if one system of religion or ethics were better than the other. Nowhere is the difference between the faiths more provocatively set down than in one of Jesus' most famous sayings, as recorded in the Gospel of Matthew 5:38: "You have heard that it hath been said 'an eye for an eye and a tooth for a tooth.' But I say unto you, resist not evil; but whosoever shall smite thee on thy right cheek, turn to him the other."

I have always taken great pains to remind non-Jewish

audiences unfamiliar with the historical background of the biblical period to understand that the much-misunderstood biblical principle of "an eye for an eye" was *never* carried out literally. What it meant, as it was actually practiced in ancient times, was fair and just and equal payment in *money* for any bodily damages—plain and simple financial compensation for bodily injury.

As with so many other examples of Old Testament legislation, what appears on the *surface* of the text to be primitive and heartless was, in truth, just the reverse. This routine, everyday ancient practice represented, in fact, a totally new, bold, and revolutionary breakthrough along a radically different and more humanistic moral direction in ancient times. The example of capital punishment is yet another dramatic example of actually liberalizing and humanizing the moral law. There is no hiding the fact that capital punishment *is* to be found explicitly in the biblical text. In actual practice, however, ancient Jewish legal commentaries on the biblical text reveal that capital punishment was administered so rarely that a single instance in a period of seventy years was regarded as an unusual occurrence. I have always gone out of my lecturing way to clarify these points with non-Jewish audiences because early on I discovered that a great deal of Christian interpretation of the Jewish Bible consciously or unconsciously taught the faithful that it was not until the emergence of Jesus and the writers of the New Testament, nineteen hundred years ago, that a higher and more inspired order of ethical sensitivity and moral nobility became the norm for proper human and religious behavior. Ironically, one has only to examine the actual practice of criminal law in Christian society down through the ages to realize that gentile legal conduct throughout history has been at sharp if not hypocritical variance from Jesus' original message mandating turning the other cheek and loving one's enemy.

Where many Christians unfamiliar with Judaism still tend to misunderstand the basic thrust of Jewish ethics is in their reading of what appears to be an unrelenting Old Testament emphasis upon negative ethical warnings. Time and again in the Jewish Bible one reads of *not* doing this and *not* doing that. Most of the famous Ten Commandments are similarly phrased in this forbidding, negative, declarative manner: thou shalt not steal, thou shalt not murder, thou shalt not covet, thou shalt not lie, and so on. In fact, of the 613 commandments in the Mosaic Law, only 248 of the laws are what could be called positive commandments, whereas 365 of the laws are unmistakably negative commandments.

One of the most famous negative mandates in all of ancient Jewish literature, for that matter, was uttered by one of the most revered sages of Jewish history, Hillel, who was a contemporary of Jesus. Hillel commanded in his famous golden rule: "Do not do unto others what is hateful for yourself." It is more or less common knowledge that Jesus phrased the same moral mandate not negatively but positively: "Do unto others what you would have others do unto you." Clearly, there is room here for some confusion and misunderstanding. My own explanation has always been to explain the difference between Hillel and Jesus so as to have non-Jews focus on the more compelling moral question: why does Judaism emphasize the negative rather than the positive?

First of all, any fair and objective understanding of the Jewish Bible should make it crystal-clear that the Mosaic law was never meant to set up humanly *un*workable moral and ethical mandates. The writers of ancient Jewish scripture and the rabbis who followed them for centuries were among the first ethical teachers in the field of religion to keenly recognize the natural human weaknesses and moral foibles of the average man and woman. And, because of this fundamental recognition of human failing and moral imperfection, the biblical and rabbinical legal tradition was determined to set before each and every Jew a practical, down-to-earth, and wholly achievable system of daily do-able ethical behavior. To demand of average people that they turn their cheek when someone abuses them, this, in the cold light of day, Judaism declares, was the absolute height of human unreality, if not stupidity. To believe that we can *love* the same people who make our lives miserable, Judaism has always argued, is a totally ridiculous, if not impossible, human response.

Is it not far more mature and down-to-earth, when it comes to dealing with our enemies, our Jewish forefathers instructed us, to heed the more compelling advice given in Proverbs 24:17: "Rejoice not when thine enemy falleth, and let not thy heart be glad or gloat when he stumbleth, lest the Lord see it and it displease Him." Elsewhere in the Book of Proverbs, the classic Jewish ethical approach states humanely: "If thine enemy be hungry, give him bread to eat; and if he be thirsty, give him water to drink." Human nature being what it is, even such elementary human decency and compassion for the enemy is still, quite honestly, superhuman. However, the Jewish ethical tradition believes that it is not beyond the bounds of human capacity, decency, and experience.

I have time and again found, in discussing this compelling subject, that many Christian eyes and ears, when exposed to Judaism's negative perspective on this matter, have been opened wide and sympathetically to the differences here between Hillel and Jesus. It no longer becomes an impossible religious stretch for many sensitive non-Jews to recognize the compelling and practical wisdom of this strikingly different Jewish point of view. What we have here is a bold but clearly understandable perspective which states, simply but powerfully, that while we may not be able to do everything to our neighbor that we would like our neighbor to do unto us, at least there must be greater moral merit in focusing, first and foremost, upon *not* doing anything to our neighbor which is at heart essentially deceitful and unworthy in our own eyes. Putting it even more bluntly: if you have to decide what is your prime ethical duty in this life, as viewed from the perspective of either Jesus or Hillel, any really open-minded non-

Jew could easily switch moral gears here and recognize, without too much difficulty, that our *cardinal* ethical duty in this life is not to love our neighbor as we love ourselves; but rather, whether Christian or Jew, to focus long and hard on trying to develop and cultivate the basic virtue of ethical *restraint*. Judaism challenges Jew and Christian not to oppress our neighbor, not to deceive him, and not to impose our own self-centered ideas or personal way of living upon our neighbor. If human beings can manage to achieve just *this* much in inter-personal human relations—that is to say, if we can discipline ourselves not to do any demeaning, debasing, and despicable things to each other— then most of us could assuredly agree that a giant ethical step forward by all of us can be taken in this life.

I have attempted to drive home this religious point so that non-Jews will come to see that this contrasting kind of religious advice is not tantamount to entering the house of good conduct through the ethical backdoor. Judaism is graphically stressing here that instead of concentrating on being *good*, we should, in effect, be reminding ourselves not to be bad. None of us, of course, will ever really be able to attain perfect ethical behavior in this life. But, who among us, Christian or Jew, cannot exert far better, far stronger, and far more meaningful control over our basic human nature and behavior? Another ancient Jewish sage raised the same basic moral question that still commands our combined Christian-Jewish attention today: "Who is the truly successful person in this life? He who controls his own passions, as it is said in the Bible: `He that is slow to anger is better than the Almighty; and he that hath mastery over his own nature is mightier than he that taketh a city' "(Chapters of the Fathers 4:1).

15

Better You Should Have Chosen Some Other People!
(or, What Does It Really Mean to Be Chosen by God?)

Over the centuries, various statements and ideas recorded in the Jewish Bible that mean one very specific and noble thing to us Jews have been given an entirely different and highly negative anti-Jewish interpretation by non-Jews. Some of this has been due to deliberate falsification. But most of this kind of defamation of Jews and Judaism, I sincerely believe, has been the result of sheer lack of knowledge. In discussing the concept of "an eye for an eye" in an earlier chapter, I pointed out that this ancient law of retaliation was totally twisted out of shape, meaning, and reality. It was taken as but a dramatic and outrageous example of Judaism's essentially being a religion of vengeance, cruelty, and cold-hearted impersonal justice. Whereas Christianity, by comparison, as evidenced by the moral charge of Jesus in the New Testament, went on record as urging people that "whosoever shall smite thee on thy right cheek, turn to him the other." In other words, Christianity presents itself as a religion highlighting nonresistance, forgiveness, love, and a higher level of justice that is always tempered by mercy.

This "eye for an eye" dilemma pales into insignificance whenever I focus upon the Jewish biblical idea of chosenness in my interfaith teaching and dialoguing. While there are virtually no Old Testament references to an ancient belief in a personal life after death, I remind my non-Jewish audiences that there are references galore in the Jewish Bible where God clearly and triumphantly designates the people of Israel as having been specifically "chosen." In countless biblical passages, including Deuteronomy 10:15 and 26:18–19, Isaiah 42 and 43, Amos 3:2, and Ezekiel 20:5–6, as well as throughout the Jewish prayer book, it is clearly and dramatically implied, if not asserted, that there is an original covenant, pact (or *berit* in Hebrew) between God and the Jewish people.

What seems, however, to have been lost in the translation or in the subsequent non-Jewish interpretation, is that the specific terms of the covenantal contract between God and Israel *never* meant that being chosen by God brought the Jews superior privileges or an elite status. God's so-called choosing, also known as the election of Israel, originally meant, and still does three thousand years later, that we Jews accepted a supreme divine challenge to fulfill God's will by taking on, in every generation, certain very specific moral and spiritual demands and obligations.

Those who seek to defame and denigrate Jews and Judaism have unceasingly attempted over the centuries to interpret the idea of chosenness conferred upon the Jewish people as a special status of *group_*superiority, privilege, and exclusivity. Alleged Jewish clannishness over the ages has thus been explained by the unthinking and prejudiced as originating from the idea of divine election, which allegedly motivates Jews in every generation to regard themselves as better than non-Jews.

An objective study of the last nineteen centuries of ancient and modern Jewish persecution, exile, and mass martyrdom should explode the long-standing myth of the Jew as being the treasured, protected, chosen darling of the divine. If being thus "selected" brings the horrendous, continuing tragedy that has befallen the Jewish people past and present, spare us such dubious honors!

In attempting to enlighten the average non-Jewish audience to regard the ancient concept of Jews as a chosen people in a more factual, positive, and honest manner, as Jews themselves have always understood it, I stress that Jews relate to the biblical idea of their chosenness, uniqueness, and difference as a proud acknowledgment that our ancestors, at the dawn of history, made unique and pioneering revolutionary contributions to Middle Eastern and Western civilization. Many other peoples, ancient and modern, have made equally great and path-breaking contributions: the Greeks in philosophy, the Romans in law, the English in literature, Americans in constitutional democracy. What we Jews pioneered in the realm of religion is, we believe, unquestionably our most momentous group contribution. In this regard, the ushering in of the idea of monotheism by Abraham and his descendants, as refined and developed by Moses and the Hebrew prophets, is, in our accounting, the most electrifying contribution the Jews have made. That we Jews were somehow pre-ordained to launch the breakthrough concept of one God into the pagan world is really not the core consideration. We believe that it just occurred that way, and we are quite elated to take the credit.

What is equally important to acknowledge is that as one moves on to the later stages of Jewish history, we Jews have never been shy in looking upon the Jewish Bible itself as constituting one of the most remarkable literary and spiritual documents to emerge from the hand and heart of any people on earth. Within its pages are to be found, shared and beloved by non-Jews, the core mandate for pioneering institutions like the Sabbath, the Holiness Code for all faiths inscribed in Leviticus 19, Hebrew prophecy defining and dictating for all humankind the moral essence of all true religion, psalms encapsulating humanity's ultimate praise for the Almighty, and the inspired faith of the biblical Job heralding the ultimate human embrace of the divine. Over the years of my career, I have relished trumpeting before non-Jews that these contributions represent only the "short list" of our people's utterly unique and enduring contributions to history—contributions that we Jews unashamedly believe we were mysteriously yet gloriously chosen—or destined, if you will—to produce.

Mystery or no, let no Jew or non-Jew ever minimize these unique Jewish achievements. They stem from no claim of ours of any higher Jewish wisdom or group arrogance, but from a deep and profound awareness that our ancestors were poised, somehow, on the cutting edge of certain breakthrough religious and moral insights. Why we Jews, rather than some other equally worthy people, were chosen to be the bearers of this new ethical and spiritual light, remains for us a permanent mystery and fascination. The interreligious bottom line, however, is that chosenness and our other contributions are basic historical facts in which Jews unapologetically take enormous pride.

16

How Can a Gentile Cope with Jewish History?
(or, What Christians Have to Learn About Christian Anti-Semitism)

Even Jews who are conversant with the long, tortured history of the Jewish people have a very difficult time trying to make sense of the incredibly unending phenomenon of anti-Semitism. In teaching Jewish history to non-Jews throughout years of conversion-class lectures and pulpit preachment, I realized that most Roman Catholics and Protestants find it almost impossible to absorb the depth, extent, and overpowering reality of Christian anti-Semitism and what it has meant to Jews and what it has done to Jews. Many of my non-Jewish students confessed shock and shame upon being first exposed to this gruesome history. So many more asked me: "How could the Jewish people have survived this continuing and crushing history? The question above questions with which they wrestled was: "Rabbi, in the face of this endless assault, what has enabled the Jewish people to remain intact as a group and carry on creatively as a vital religious presence today in our Western and Middle Eastern civilization?"

It is far easier to answer the second question before the first. In the Middle Ages, when Christian society first locked up the Jews in tight ghetto quarters, cutting them off from the mainstream of Christian life, Jews miraculously managed to create for themselves, behind the ghetto walls, a rich, deep, and strengthening religious and cultural environment that fostered group literacy and scholarship from infancy to adulthood. Jewish brain power, for centuries denied normal access to European culture and society, channeled its great intellectual resources into the unique spiritual and religious literature of the Jewish past. This almost total Jewish intellectual preoccupation for centuries with the Bible and postbiblical Jewish literature and law was directly responsible for producing an almost unbroken chain of passionate students of Jewish law and enraptured lovers of Jewish learning and Jewish culture. In the midst of a vast European desert of mass popular ignorance and illiteracy, the humblest Jewish ghetto was a veritable oasis of literacy and enlightenment. History, however, shows that if you situate a Jew in a basically raw and totally uncultured non-ghetto environment, the same Jew in time could well become as unresponsive to learning as anyone from any other group similarly situated.

What I have energetically tried to convey to Christian audiences over my career is that we Jews are *not* a religion. It is infinitely more accurate to understand that we Jews *have* a religion. We have a religion that speaks out to us and to other religions, compellingly and triumphantly, even under the worst of Christian pressure. Not just for the last nineteen centuries, but for thirty centuries and more, we Jews have had a religion that stands for reason and intellect over superstition and thought control, for a universal ethic as opposed to a clan morality, and for a realistic emphasis upon the moral challenge of *this* world as against the *next*. We Jews have a religion that stands primarily for hope and faith as against resignation and despair. From Judaism's point of view, these historic ideals and imperatives have been and still are the basic religious tools of our Jewish survival. And they inspiringly answer for us the age-old question as to how to accurately define group and individual Jewish identity.

Going back to my initial question of helping non-Jews to get a proper read on Christian responsibility for anti-Semitism, I have tried consistently to make it a priority for the average Christian student in learning about Jewish history to realize that prejudice against Jews and Judaism falls into two distinct and prolonged periods of world history. Obviously, what comes to mind first, in non-Jewish memory are the two thousand years of Christian history. During this more recent period, the absolute worst of anti-Semitism occurred.

Long before the time of Jesus, however, unbeknown to many Christians, there existed a pre-Christian era of still another thousand years of Jewish history where the term "anti-Semitism" was unknown. In its ugly place, however, there existed a powerful anti-Jewishness or anti-Judaism that differed markedly from later Christian anti-Semitism. This early form of anti-Jewishness centered chiefly around the millennial clash between the monotheistic religion of the ancient Hebrews and the pagan religious worship embraced by all of Israel's idol-worshipping neighbors. For a thousand years before Christianity arrived on the scene, ancient Israel's most deadly battles were against the might of the pagan world empires of Egypt, Assyria, Babylon, Persia, Greece, and Rome. During this pre-Christian millennium there was an unending clash of violently competing ancient religious cultures that can in no way be compared with the Christian variety of church-inspired anti-Semitism that has dogged the last twenty centuries of Jewish existence.

With its new status in the fourth century as the official state religion of the Roman Empire, Christianity took over the role of oppressing and demonizing Jews and Judaism. Much of this demonization first reared its ugly head in countless passages in the New Testament that were used by the early church to depict all Jews as hostile to Jesus, if not actual Christ-killers. The church fathers went out of their way, down through the generations, to drum home the deadly thesis that the Jew, because of his rejection of Christ, was inevitably lost and doomed to eternal pariah status and fully deserving, in the eyes and teaching of the church, of endless and justifiable persecution.

The late Middle Ages saw a continuing frenzy of hate and discrimination against the Jews. During this period, Jews were physically isolated from the mainstream of Christian Europe through forced ghettoization where Jews were subjected to non-stop persecution and ultimately to expulsion from the Christian countries of their origin. The most infamous of these expulsions took place in England and France during the thirteenth and fourteenth centuries and in Spain and Portugal in the 1490s. In the early Middle Ages, Christian crusaders added still another black chapter to Jewish martyrdom. On their inspired way to wrest the Holy Land from Moslem control, the crusaders savaged and decimated a chain of small Jewish communities along their route to Jerusalem. This crusading anti-Jewish insanity was fomented, more often than not, by overzealous clergymen, avaricious nobles, and deeply prejudiced masses. All of this twisted religious passion was the inevitable outgrowth of the previous centuries of distortion and perversion during which Christian Europe was unremittingly brainwashed into believing the absolute worst about the Jews and Judaism.

Anti-Semitism was relieved somewhat with the coming of the Protestant Reformation and the American and French revolutions, which attempted to engender a desperately needed spirit of religious toleration into Christian European society. The Jews in Western European countries during the nineteenth century began to enjoy some significant political, economic, and cultural freedoms. But Jews in Eastern European countries, under the tyrannical rule of the tsars, continued to suffer grievous oppression. Russian anti-Semitism became so intolerable by the end of the nineteenth century that nearly three million Jews fled the Russian Empire and emigrated to the United States between 1880 and 1924. Here, in America, Jews were

finally able to attain the freedoms they had been systematical-
ly denied for well over a thousand years in Christian Europe.

In the latter part of my rabbinical career, I encountered new
generations of non-Jews who were shocked to learn that one of
the most intense periods of anti-Semitism had occurred in our
very own country during the 1930s. My students were amazed
to learn that the Great Depression of the 1930s, which tore
American society apart, also created intense anti-Semitism and
Jewish scapegoating that saw raw, ugly, and open discrimination against Jews in academe, corporate America, and the marketplace in general. Once the United States was drawn into the
war against the Japanese and the Germans in 1941, the country's war effort became directly instrumental in helping to
break down a good many of the shameful barriers of religious
discrimination, thereby finally making it possible for American
Jews to go as far as their talents, opportunities, and dreams
took them. In the postwar era, America became a "golden age"
for the country's Jewish community in terms of Jewish ease
and acceptability in a society still overwhelmingly Christian.

It was difficult to give my non-Jewish audiences, whether I
was teaching in a classroom setting or speaking from a church
pulpit, an emotional feel for American anti-Semitism in the
1930s. My greatest frustration even to this very day has been to
awaken and sensitize non-Jewish audiences to the crushing
reality of the tragedy of tragedies that befell European Jewry
during the now-distant period of World War II. In retelling the
horrific scope of the Holocaust, I would always preface my
narrative with an admission that I knew in my heart how
almost impossible it was for people unfamiliar with the grim
history of that nightmarish era to relate personally to the
destruction of one-third of the Jewish people during the Nazi
period. In presenting the Holocaust story to the average non-
Jewish audience, I also always prefaced my remarks by saying
that we are all stunned when confronting a rifle-toting mass
murderer who guns down a handful of innocent campus stu-

dents. We all recoil with genuine horror and disbelief in the face of an Oklahoma City terrorist bombing that destroyed the lives of scores of innocents. A single child trapped in a deep well automatically catches us all by the throat. The downing of an airliner in Scotland, or off Long Island, with total instant loss of all human life aboard—all these types of deaths, I assured them, instinctively grab our immediate attention and instant sympathy. I also reminded my audiences, both non-Jewish and Jewish, that war monuments like the Vietnam Memorial Wall in Washington, can induce us to relate dramatically to the sickening magnitude of tragic death on the scale of thousands upon thousands of our countrymen. And then I unashamedly confess my total inability to draw a mental or verbal picture of a million and a half Jewish children force-marched to their deaths in German concentration camps and in the ovens of Dachau and Treblinka. Not to mention drawing another scarifying image of the parallel mass liquidation of another four million of their parents and grandparents.

Over half a century has passed since World War II, and with the coming of the twenty-first century I still break out in a sweat as I periodically relive my people's horror, whether in my own fevered historical memory or in the pedagogic context of trying to teach a new generation, Jewish and non-Jewish, about the Holocaust. In addressing gentile groups, I must also confess that my hidden agenda has always been to document for them how centuries and centuries of Catholic and Protestant anti-Jewish preaching, teaching, and demonization inevitably paved the way for this greatest of all of tragedies in the four thousand years of Jewish history. I have also wanted my non-Jewish listeners to realize that in European country after country controlled by the Germans, the diabolic plan to exterminate the native Jewish population met with enthusiastic support, if not relish, among an entire continent of non-Germanic sympathizers whose native conscious and unconscious anti-Jewishness was inbred by centuries of church and lay discrimination against the Jews. I have wanted to make it easy and logical for them to understand how Hitler so smoothly and cleverly tapped into this built-in hatred and prejudice against Jews and Judaism which can be traced all the way back to the first century C.E., when, with the emergence of the daughter faith of Judaism, the demonization of Judaism and the Jew took root and took off.

I have taken great pains to demonstrate that anti-Semitism, to be sure, also had roots in many nonreligious facets of Christian civilization. Yet I stress that newcomers to Judaism and Jewish history have to understand where the main and most devastating responsibility for anti-Semitism lies, and how this scourge continues to anguish every Jew and to diminish every non-Jew.

Along with chronicling the anti-Semitic evils that have transpired for centuries, I have always attempted to leave my students with some hope that their generation and successive generations of Christians can and will see radically new and more positive attitudes emerging between Christian and Jew. I genuinely want non-Jews to appreciate the sea changes stirring in the modern Catholic Church. The revolutionary and compassionate papacies of John XXIII in the 1960s and John Paul in the 1990s, I explain to students and potential converts, represent breakthrough religious challenges confronting the Catholic clergy and Catholic masses. Here, at last, are unprecedented papal declarations to all Catholics and all true Christians acknowledging that the core evil of Christian anti-Semitism is nothing less than a basic sacrilege against Christ himself and all of Christianity.

Some liberal Protestant churches have also come to the belated realization that very few Christian communities were able to escape the contagion of anti-Judaism and its modern successor, anti-Semitism. It gives me some comfort to feel that at least Catholics and Protestants are finally beginning to recognize that the historic scourge of anti-Semitism is, at heart, a sinful contradiction and a basic affront to the Christian Gospel, which positively demands a dramatic new reading and reinterpretation.

Notwithstanding these promising and almost messianically healing interfaith overtures, I have never left my students or potential converts under any illusion that Christian anti-Semitism, inculcated for nineteen long centuries, is capable of disappearing overnight or even ever. Jews must realize that the majority of non-Jews probably will never ever personally relate to this long grim history and come to see anti-Semitism for what it has horribly done to the Jew, and what essentially remains for Christians and Christianity to undo if any major breakthrough and dramatically new interreligious understanding and respect can ever emerge.

17

How One Jew Can Instinctively Spot Another

(or, Why Are Jews Recognizable to One Another?)

Jews historically have characterized themselves not as a racial group or a national entity but more as a social *type,* a people whose members are acutely aware of each other. This powerful sense of social belonging has been sharpened for all Jews by the cementing bond of centuries-old persecution and by the intoxication of group survival in the face of historic suffering. That is to say, our Jewishness, as we perceive it, is no blind drive of blood, race, or tribe. Jews are what they are primarily because of their centuries-old absorption of a self-conscious Jewish culture accompanied by a historically handed down code of moral, ethical, and ritual priorities.

We Jews believe that we are not to be classified primarily as a race or a nation, notwithstanding the emergence in the mid-twentieth century of the State of Israel. There is still a mysterious degree of ethnic singularity among Jews to which we most often respond instinctively. That is to say, there seems to be a gut recognition among us Jews such that wherever we may confront one other, we seem to be very much alike in mood, manner, and habit of mind. The reason for this, I believe, touches upon the factor of environment. While hereditary physical characteristics are certainly one major influence determining human life and personality, the factor of environment is an even more impressive influence that accounts for many of the mutual resemblances among Jews and is the source of many typically Jewish characteristics.

A key sociological factor that has deeply influenced the Jewish group is the fact that for well over the last thousand years, Jews have generally been city dwellers. The urbanization of the Jewish people has undoubtedly had a significant effect upon our physical stature, our basic emotional mood, and our intellectual temperament. Like all city-dwellers in our Western civilization, Jews were prone to be quick-witted, somewhat cynical, and highly sophisticated in comparison with the generally slow-paced, reflective, and less cultured inhabitants of rural areas.

The Jews, however, were not your *average* city-dwellers. Even in the city, our ancestors were forced to live under bizarre and restrictive circumstances. For centuries, up until the nineteenth century, our people were locked out of the European handicraft guilds and artisan professions by the church and the government. In the Middle Ages, Jews were actually forced by church canon law to take up the despised commercial activity of moneylending and financial investment. As a result of this being the only allowable avenue of commerce open to the European Jew, the shrewdness and cunning normally associated with this type of commercial venture attached itself to the Jews as a community. What most non-Jews, however, fail to acknowledge is that the great medieval period of forced Jewish moneylending coincided dramatically with the mass erection of cathedrals and monasteries, hundreds of which were built and financed mainly by European Jewish enterprise. Indeed, many other notable advances in the field of European commerce, industry, colonization, and culture were daringly conceived, endorsed, and supported by pioneering Jewish moneylending ventures.

Jews managed, more importantly, to create for themselves behind the walls of the ghetto a rich, deep, and strengthening *cultural* environment fostering literacy, thoughtfulness, and scholarship from infancy to adulthood. Jewish brain-power, denied access for centuries to the normal avenues of European culture and society, channeled its resources into the great spiritual and religious history of the Jewish past. This almost total intellectual preoccupation for centuries with the Bible and postbiblical Jewish literature and law was uniquely responsible for producing an unbroken chain of passionate students of Jewish law and enraptured lovers of Jewish learning and culture. In the midst of a vast medieval European desert of mass ignorance and illiteracy, the humblest Jewish ghetto was a veritable oasis of literacy, culture, and enlightenment.

When the Jewish national home of Judea was totally destroyed by the Romans nineteen hundred years ago, Judaism kept the Jewish people intact and viable. Over the ages, whenever any national group was destroyed, the people belonging to that nation, bereft of army, navy, royalty, land, commerce, and coinage, generally disappeared forever from the stage of history. Not so with the Jewish people who even though in a state of seemingly endless and hopeless physical exile, incredibly bounded back from their loss of nation and land. They were able to maintain their group solidarity and integrity through the exclusive vehicle of their *religion*. In the place of national law, the religious laws of the Bible and the Talmud prevailed. In the place of national authority, the authority of the rabbis provided definitive legal and social leadership. The religious calendar of the Jewish faith provided memorable soul-lifting festivals, holy days, and rituals that nourished and richly sustained the Jews in their long dark exile. They were thus invested with an imperishable will to carry on as a clearly viable group steadfastly committed to the ideals and aspiration of their religion.

When all is said and done, it would be more accurate to state that we Jews are not a *religion*. It would be more accurate to say that we Jews *have* a religion. We have a religion that has spoken out to us and to other religions compellingly and triumphantly for over thirty centuries. We have had and still have a religion that stands for reason and intellect over superstition and thought control. We have a religion that historically has espoused a universal ethic as opposed to a clan morality. Our religion places a realistic emphasis upon the central moral and ethical challenge of *this* world as against the next. Our religion opts for hope and faith over resignation and despair. All of these Jewish ideals and imperatives, we believe, have been and still are the basic and essential tools promoting Jewish survival. In addition, they represent the indisputable answer to the age-old question of how to define Jewish identity and decide who is a Jew.

18

From "God Is In His Holy Temple" to "Deidle Deidle Dee Dum Deidle Deidle Dee"
(or, What Separates Old-Time Reform Judaism from Modern Day Mainstream Reform?)

In June of 1951, when I was ordained as a Reform rabbi from the Hebrew Union College–Jewish Institute of Religion in New York, the Reform movement in America was on the threshold of a physical and religious explosion. Before the beginning of World War II, the number of Reform congregations in the United States was as few as 250. Within a decade and a half, our movement tripled to about 750 congregations embracing almost a million members. Most of this new congregational growth took place in the suburbs of New York, Philadelphia, Chicago, Los Angeles, and other major metropolitan cities where postwar housing was booming and brand-new Jewish communities were springing up overnight. Every one of my rabbinical school classmates, upon ordination from the New York School, stepped into these brand-new congregations, located mainly in the Greater New York area. During our seminary years, as part of our practical rabbinical experience, each Sabbath weekend rabbinical students would travel to these new suburban communities in Long Island, Westchester,

Connecticut, and New Jersey and provide desperately needed rabbinic leadership for these fast-growing infant Reform synagogues.

I was the only member of my graduating class who chose to begin his rabbinical career not in one of these brand-new suburban congregations but as an assistant rabbi in a huge old-line classical Reform temple in Pittsburgh, Pennsylvania that had been founded in 1854. Before my ordination, I had been invited to accept the pulpit of a new congregation in the process of being organized in Washington, D.C. It was a very tempting maiden rabbinical opportunity, which seemed at the time to perfectly suit my rabbinical temperament and dreams. I turned the Washington congregation's offer down, however, because I believed that by going to Pittsburgh and becoming assistant rabbi there to a legendary giant in our profession, Solomon B. Freehof, I would have an opportunity comparable to a law school graduate clerking for a Brandeis or a Holmes on the Supreme Court. This was truly a once-in-a-lifetime rabbinical experience, and I felt that I could not possibly pass it up. I believed further that three or four years under Freehof's stellar tutelage at the very beginning of my rabbinical career would make me a better and more seasoned young rabbi when the time inevitably came a few years later to become the rabbi of my own congregation.

The only downside of my going to Pittsburgh's Rodef Shalom Congregation in 1951 (Rabbi Freehof notwithstanding) was that the congregational practice of Reform Judaism there, I quickly discovered, was mired deep and rigidly in the old-line early-twentieth-century German Reform Jewish past—a past about 180 degrees apart from the radically different, postwar suburban-style Reform Judaism that was ushering in an exciting new version of Reform Judaism not at all appreciated by the old-line German-Jewish classical reformers. The clash between old and new Reform Jews came about right after World War II because the mass infusion of American Jews joining Reform synagogues, both old-line and suburban, was made up predominantly of second- and third-generation East European Jews whose parents and grandparents had migrated to America between 1880 and 1924. The majority of these new Reform Jews were either in rebellion against the Orthodoxy of their own growing up or they were uncomfortable with Conservative synagogues, which they felt were too traditional for their modern lives, or else they felt that the Reform movement would better satisfy their modern liberal, social, and personal religious needs.

The tension between the old-line German and the new East European Reform members was sharpest and most volatile in the historic Pittsburgh-type Rodef Shalom congregations. Despite being inundated by East European Jews during the late 1940s and the 1950s, German-Jewish lay leaders and classically oriented rabbis, even as late as 1951, still tightly controlled the spiritual and ritual life of the temple. The newcomers, while welcome to swell congregational membership and income, had to conform completely to the way Reform Judaism had been instituted and was still carried on faithfully by German-Jewish preferences and practice. The classical style of Reform Judaism in the old-line temples was virtually locked into the guidelines and customs of a late-nineteenth-century Reform Jewish platform of guiding principles and practices. The Reform Movement's pioneering Pittsburgh guidelines of 1885 and the later Columbus Platform of 1937 together affirmed that *ethics* and not *ritual* was the essence and central glory of Judaism generally and of Reform Judaism in particular.

I came smack up against this ethical and ritual divide almost immediately upon beginning my assistant rabbinical duties with Rabbi Freehof at Rodef Shalom. When I asked Rabbi Freehof to recommend a place for me to buy my first black pulpit robe, he informed me, "At Rodef Shalom, my boy, we don't wear robes. Pulpit dress *here* is the formal cutaway coat and striped trousers!" My first Shabbat on the pulpit of the awesome Byzantine-style Rodef Shalom Temple, clad in that turn-of-the-century Reform ministerial get-up, I kept thinking during services that morning: "If only my Seminary classmates could see me now in this monkey suit!"

Pulpit dress for our postwar generation of Reform rabbis, most of whom, like myself, were veterans of World War II, was the flowing black clerical robe, a sartorial style borrowed from the Christian clergy. When I left Rodef Shalom four years later to assume the rabbinate of Pittsburgh's first suburban Reform congregation, I quickly ditched the cutaway tails, vest, and striped pants. Since even the robe was too "churchy" for my personal Jewish pulpit taste, I decided to wear only a simple and very conservative, dark black business suit on and off the pulpit, and that is what I did for the next thirteen years in my suburban Pittsburgh pulpit.

Lo and behold, in 1968, when I was called to the pulpit of the historic Congregation Beth Israel in New England, a Rodef Shalom–type old-line Reform temple founded way back in 1843, the pulpit dress of the rabbinate in Connecticut, I was unhappy to see, was the flowing black clerical robe, which I quickly decided to resist wearing any longer. To my great surprise, my predecessor in West Hartford, who had occupied my new pulpit for forty-three years, sported a colorful (tallis-like) narrow stole with fringes on his shoulders. This priestly stole, popular on Catholic altars, was fast beginning to make its pulpit appearance wrapped around Reform rabbinical shoulders in the postwar period. It added a bit of high color to the drabness of the black academic robe and enabled some traditionally inclined Reform rabbis to have a more traditional rabbinical public image.

Most Reform rabbis of my postwar generation were still philosophically and deliberately bare-headed in the pulpit. It has taken a full generation and more since my ordination for a rapidly growing number of younger Reform rabbis to add the traditional yarmulke to their pulpit dress. Gone now, too, are the pseudo-tallis-like stoles. Today, in main-stream Reform, one not only sees a veritable blizzard of pulpit yarmulkes but also the wearing of the traditional full-scale fringed tallis by rabbis and cantors. It will not be too long in the distant Reform future, I predict, before most of the laity will take their syna-gogue dress cues from a very traditionally garbed twenty-first-century Reform clergy.

While the classical, old-line reformers well knew that they were taking great if not radical liberties with the past, they believed that the Jewishness of their modern lives should be judged not upon scrupulous observance of the biblical law and its ancient commandments but upon their individual fidelity to Reform Judaism's more crucial and loftier demands in the area of moral and ethical obligation and com-mitment. Nineteenth and early twentieth-century Reform stressed allegiance first and foremost to the historic Hebrew prophetic call for justice, mercy, and compassion as the sin-gular hallmarks for living a proper and inspired modern Jewish life. Ritual and ceremonial practices, of and by them-selves, were never deliberately meant to be dismissed out of hand by the early reformers. They were, rather, to be regard-ed as of lesser religious importance than moral and ethical commitment. Ideally, classical Reform declared that a fine-tuned religious *balance* must be struck in this life between morality and ceremony. Reform Judaism declared that unless this balance was tipped heavily in favor of conscientiously living the moral life, fidelity to ritual alone could oftentimes border upon mere sham and show.

The big problem, however, that confronted German Jews in the classical period of pre–World War II Reform was that the Jewishness of their home and synagogue lives became virtual-ly nonexistent or paper-thin at best. Modernizing the faith in the heady climate of nineteenth-century American religious freedom led the early reformers, unfortunately, to the almost total scrapping of traditional Jewish customs and norms. What replaced them, unfortunately, was a Judaism and a Jewish lifestyle that proved to be unrecognizably Jewish. It was not only the classical Reform image of a bare-headed, tallis-free clergy ministering to gender-mixed pews. It was the virtually Hebrew-less liturgical worship. It was the prayer book deliberately switched from the traditional right-to-left-hand opening and replete with King James–style poetic English translations of the standard Hebrew text. It was the organ-pumping, Protestant-sounding hymnology that replaced the traditional closing synagogue hymns like Ein Keloheinu with "God Is in His Holy Temple." It was the nonscriptural Sunday-morning literary and social action lectures in place of the cyclical Saturday-morning biblical portion of the week. It was the Sunday school curricula worlds away from the unisex Jewish education of the cheder. It was the French horn replacing the ram's horn for trumpeting on the Jewish New Year. It was Yom Kippur sans breast-beating and fasting. It was the egg-nogging and Christmas tree trimming 'round the "Hanukkah bush." It was in-your-face sandwich-munching during Passover week. It was the thirteen-year-old (later sixteen-year-old) Bar Mitzvah–style coming of age pageantry of Confirmation ushering in Jewish young adulthood for both male and female.

Even though many of the Reform Jews I grew up with in the Rabbi Stephen Wise Temple in New York City, and in the two other classical Reform temples I served during my rabbinical career in Pittsburgh and West Hartford, were deliberately Yiddishkeit-free (totally removed from any semblance of ritual Jewishness), there were still impressive numbers of God-infused and ethically motivated Reform Jews in the Reform movement nationwide who were very proud of their historic Jewish connection. The blanket charge leveled against Reform Jews by traditional Jews of being assimilationists at heart or simply goyim at worst was not totally justified. On the other hand, in this pre–World War II phase of classical Reform, the movement, as it was perceived and practiced, was a very short and much too comfortable step for many Reform Jews to the Unitarian Church and the Ethical Culture movement, wherein humanism reigned supreme, liberalism was deified, Jesus and the church were soft-pedaled, and anything that smacked of Jewish particularism and ceremony was scorned.

Ironically, had East European Jews in the post–World War II period not poured into the old-line German Jewish Reform congregations across America in such huge numbers, the old German-style classical Reform would actually have been in serious danger of disappearing by 1945 as a major Jewish movement in the United States. In a dramatic sense, not only did American Jews of Russian, Polish, Lithuanian, Hungarian, and Romanian ancestry rescue the German-American Reform movement from marginalization if not oblivion, but it was the East European infusion that was directly responsible for moving Reform away from its classical period into what may be described as its initial mainstream period, the very time when I began my rabbinate on the heels of the post-Holocaust era, and the thrilling period of the emergence of the State of Israel.

While American Jews of East European background wanted no part of Old World or even New World Orthodoxy, they wanted their new religious ties to the Reform movement, Germanic though they were, to incorporate *some* of the positive things from their traditional family and synagogue backgrounds in the Old World which still resonated warmly with Jewishly enhancing and endearing memories. They wanted the Reform Movement, for example, to offer the long-ago-dropped ritual of Bar Mitzvah to those of its new East European members who chose to have their sons experience this historic ritual, not to mention opening up equal opportunities for their daughters to go through a female *Bat* Mitzvah experience. The East European Jews quickly grew to love and appreciate the classical Reform Confirmation ritual at age sixteen for both sexes, which kept the youngsters in religious school after Bar Mitzvah for at least another three years of higher Jewish education. The Conservative Jewish movement, incidentally, pioneered Bat Mitzvah for girls in the 1920s. Conservative Judaism also saw the educational wisdom in borrowing the Reform Confirmation ceremony and incorporating it directly into its curriculum.

The biggest headache for Reform Judaism and Conservative Judaism, however, is that in the last fifty years they have both had to confront the scandalous American Jewish phenomenon of the rampant Bar and Bat Mitzvah post-Shabbat service *social* spectacular. Herein many Jewish parents of the past several generations have felt pressured to produce luncheon and dinner entertainment extravaganzas that outorgy the worst of ancient pagan excess. What American rabbi of the past few decades cannot come up with Bar and Bat Mitzvah horror stories where the simple and historical "kichel and herring" with schnapps Bar Mitzvah reception of old has segued into a Las Vegas Night production for disco-driven, hormonally hopped-up Jewish adolescents?

The East European Jews who flooded into the German-dominated American Reform movement after the war brought with them no happy memories of the Old cheder style Jewish education. They wanted their children of both sexes to get a solid Jewish education but within the more pedagogically appealing American Sunday school context. The problem was that the limited weekend Jewish education in the average Reform Jewish Sunday school, with virtually no parental role-modeling help from the home, has produced several generations of young American Jewish Reform illiterates. Their knowledge of Jewish history, their skills with the Hebrew language, and their emotional and ceremonial ties to the cycle of Jewish holidays are basically indifferent at best, and minimal at worst.

Respect for the institution of the rabbinate was still deeply ingrained in the new East European Reform Jews. But the "John Barrymore"-non-Torah-centered pulpiteering and Stephen Wise–like rabbinic social activism and ecumenism of the new-style modern Reform rabbi soon replaced the historically all-controlling traditional rabbi whose minor and major talmudic orientation tightly and totally dominated every facet of personal and group Jewish life, custom, and law in the Old World and in some parts of the New World as well. The German Jews particularly relished addressing their rabbis as "doctor," as if that titular academic/medical appellation were a loftier and more satisfying (i.e., less Jewish) form of clerical title.

On matters dealing with historically strict dietary and Sabbath restrictions, the East European Jews were very comfortable adjusting to a radically different and Jewishly looser style of religious living and practice, where matters of personal choice and freedom ruled the day rather than being under the gun of binding rabbinic dicta and divine mandate. It wasn't that the newcomers to Reform Judaism had lost their respect for the law; but they found in their radical new Reform affiliation a joyous opportunity to remain meaningfully Jewish in a bracingly free, modern, and noncoercive way. Unfortunately, this heady new climate of religious freedom and observance often times degenerated into a personal and group "free-for-all" which found many newcomers stripping the Reform movement clean of any Jewishly authentic semblance of meaningful ceremony, custom, and ritual.

The classical Reform synagogue service is a dramatic case in point. Its welcome brevity, music, decorum, vernacular praying, and mixed pews were all a very refreshingly different and welcome spiritual setting for those uncomfortable or unhappy or far removed from the traditional synagogue worship pattern of the past. One big problem, however, with all of the radical liturgical changes brought about by the classical Reform service was that in far too many Reform temples of the classical period, the service degenerated into a mass, almost total "spectator" kind of worship that touched, involved, and moved few. The Reform Jewish worshipper might have felt equally at home in a Unitarian, Ethical Culture, or Quaker type of religious service.

When my postwar generation of Reform rabbis came upon the early 1950s Reform Jewish scene, we realized that if the old-line style of classical Reform Judaism did not move substantially away from its bare-boned Jewishness, American Reform might well die out in less than a generation. This was actually happening in the late 1930s and early 1940s. My own congregation in West Hartford, founded back in 1843, had a century later, in 1943, involved fewer than 250 German-Jewish families at its membership peak. If not for the postwar East European infusion during the next decade, which brought into the congregation over a thousand new families, Beth Israel and the entire classical Reform movement, which was similarly exploding, would have slowly but surely remained on the periphery of American Jewish life or perhaps have completely faded away before the twentieth century came to an end.

My first classical Reform congregational experience in Pittsburgh from 1951 to 1955, at Rodef Shalom, turned out to be the most resistant of the old-line temples in the movement in its response to the dramatic sea changes that were beginning to shake up Reform Judaism. Even the great Rabbi Solomon B. Freehof, who grew up Orthodox in Baltimore, deliberately low-keyed his own traditional Jewish roots and did little or to turn his German-Jewish Reform Pittsburgh congregation away from its Jewish minimalism and basically assimilationist religious behavior. I remember getting hell from a prominent group of old-line German Jewish-families when they bitterly complained about my public and bulletin denunciations of Jewish families in the congregation having Christmas trees in their homes in December and almost totally ignoring the Hanukkah season.

Another uproar I remember was when a delegation of the old-line parents came to see me to denounce me for requiring their sons and daughters to be exposed to a minimal Hebrew-language curriculum in the primary grades of the Sunday school. This tiny but prominent group of old-line German families threatened to pull their kids out of the temple's Sunday school (which they ultimately did) and run a rump Sunday school of their own where the "offending" Hebrew-language input, Israel-related curriculum, and Christmas tree objections were all erased. Shock waves also went out to many in the congregation who reacted negatively to my encouraging members, if they so chose, to break the glass at wedding ceremonies, or to my asking religious school children to light Shabbat candles at home on Friday night, or my urging adults and children to fast on Yom Kippur, and stay home from public and private school and come to temple to worship on the festival holy days, or my effort to persuade them to refrain from eating sandwiches at home and in school during the week of Passover.

My senior colleague was clearly unhappy with my tampering with the long-established German-Jewish customs of the congregation, since it was obvious that he had chosen not to "rock the boat" during his long and esteemed tenure. To his credit, though, he never forbade me from experimenting with many of these new changes which were being introduced everywhere in our movement. His basic rabbinical style was just to steer clear of any serious controversy in the congregation. He wanted essentially to concentrate on his glittering role as master preacher, teacher, and lecturer. His chief wish was to spend most of his rabbinical hours, public and private, concentrating upon his scholarly studies and engaging in a widespread Jewish legal correspondence. Here, he was regarded as the utter master in the area of Jewish jurisprudence by adoring colleagues in and out of the Reform movement who were forever turning to him to adjudicate thorny and truly controversial Jewish legal issues touching upon provocative matters of acceptable Reform practice. One of the great ironies of this rabbinical giant, respected by all branches of the rabbinate for his scholarly and practical advice in the area of Jewish law and practice, was that, for the fast-changing and developing Reform Jewish movement, Freehof was, in essence, the ultimate guide and role-model for rabbis and lay leaders. We were all struggling mightily, a generation ago, to deal sympathetically, constructively, and radically with the best and most troubling of the Orthodox Jewish past in the hope of modifying it with Jewishly authentic and liberal accommodation.

While Freehof privately consoled himself with the knowledge that I would only be around as his assistant for a few years, and that another less controversial assistant would follow me when I moved on to assume my own pulpit in suburban Pittsburgh, we were still like father and son on many other personal and family matters, despite the issues on which I often roiled the waters during my tenure with him. The first years of my young rabbinate that I was privileged to spend with him were truly memorable. Learning *what* to do as his proud assistant influenced me greatly in the years ahead. But I must confess that learning what *not* to do, as *he* chose not to do it rabbinically, was equally critical for me to absorb and to act upon quite differently for the remainder of my rabbinate.

Mainstream Reform, besides reflecting a radically different ethnic turnover in our movement, witnessed a growingly powerful desire to inject a more significant Jewish dimension into mid-twentieth-century Reform Judaism. While the new-style East European Reform Jews found it easy and comfortable to reject traditional Jewish ideas and dogmas dealing with the Messiah, life after death, resurrection, and the binding authority of biblical and postbiblical law and rabbinic authority, they were clearly uncomfortable and unfulfilled with a Reform synagogue and a Jewish calendar and home life that were barely Jewish in content, practice, feel, and in-reach. In no way, however, did they want to go back to historical Orthodoxy.

The movement veered sharply away from German classical Reform mainly because the newcomers wanted their worship to include a Hebraic component that still resonated emotionally in their hearts and on their tongues. They hungered to hear and sing a style of synagogue music that rang with familiar moving cantillations from the past but could be blended with a cantorial dash of the new. They wanted the cycle of Jewish holy days to reconnect their liberal modern religious lives more meaningfully and more warmly with the best and richest of their past. The first wave of postwar "mainstreamers" honestly sought a solid Jewishness in Reform that would proudly honor their Jewish faith and identity and would remain a core identity they could be proud of and could pass on down to their children.

When I began my rabbinical career in 1951 on the cutting edge of this new mainstream Reform Judaism, little did I realize that almost two decades later, when I was called to assume the historic pulpit of Congregation Beth Israel in West Hartford, it would be, as baseball's Casey Stengel aptly said, "déjà vu' all over again!" I had been more or less prepared, way back in 1951, for the congregational world of German classical Reform at Rodef Shalom in Pittsburgh. But I was totally nonplussed to see that Congregation Beth Israel as late as 1968 seemed to have resisted virtually everything that was going on in our fast-changing Reform movement by way of the new mainstream changes. Prior to my coming to Beth Israel as senior rabbi, I had been knee-deep in all of these Reform changes in my post-Freehof Pittsburgh suburban congregation for the past thirteen years, where change had almost become the absolute norm throughout the movement.

Beth Israel in 1968, in fact, was a depressing throwback to the ways of the old classical German Reform congregations of the past, still rooted in what came to be known as the "classical" Reform era. What truly surprised me when I assumed the rabbinate in West Hartford was the astounding realization that the congregation's huge East European member infusion since the postwar period had had so little impact in turning the congregation away from its classical German Reform past. When I took over the pulpit in 1968, many of the old German families were still surprisingly in the leadership, even though they were now in the rapidly shrinking minority. Yet another serious roadblock I had to confront was the unexpected resistance to *any* kind of change, which was a reflection of Connecticut's legendary reputation for being "the land of steady habits."

My rude awakening to this regional phenomenon came when I urged my new ritual committee, at our first meeting upon my taking over the spiritual reins of the congregation, to change the starting time for Friday evening services. My motive was simple. In my former suburban Pittsburgh congregation, where young families predominated, I wanted to make it easier for them to have a leisurely Shabbat dinner at home and then have a little more time to get a babysitter and arrange to come to worship without killing themselves. Thus, for years in suburban Pittsburgh, we began our Friday evening congregational worship at 8:45 p.m. Even the older families, without children, appreciated the later starting time.

In West Hartford, which traditionally had begun services at 8:00 p.m. before I arrived on the scene, I figured the jump from 8:00 to 8:45 would be a radical change. Thus I recommended a compromise time of 8:15 to encourage younger members to come to worship. The battle that ensued on that minuscule time change, within the ritual committee and on the board, erupted with such mindless frenzy that you would have imagined I was proposing a major change in the congregational bylaws mandating that every Beth Israel household should henceforth become kosher overnight!

With "victory" behind me on the worship time-change, I next turned my attention to more pressing and substantive matters of congregational change in my 125-year-old classical Reform Jewish warhorse. The first significant educational change I pushed through was to advance the Confirmation rite from age fifteen to sixteen. Virtually the entire Reform movement almost a generation before had seen the wisdom of having students confirmed at this later age where they would be able to benefit immeasurably from the additional opportunity for higher and deeper Jewish education. Confirmation originally was held at age thirteen in the early nineteenth century. Generation by generation, it was advanced to sixteen. After the depressing battle over the worship service time-change, I expected a battle royal in the congregation over this truly substantive change. It never occurred.

Regarding the rite of Bar Mitzvah, which for several generations had been barely tolerated by my predecessor, I immediately made it crystal-clear to the congregation that I personally rejoiced in this historic ceremony, I set in motion curriculum plans to have the temple also offer the Bat Mitzvah rite to thirteen-year-old girls, which came to pass shortly.

A very positive spin-off of this egalitarian coming-of-age Bar/Bat Mitzvah ritual was that now and in the future both sexes were to be exposed to radically enlarged Hebrew-language studies not only in connection with Bar and Bat Mitzvah but with a new and earlier exposure to Hebrew beginning in the third grade three times a week, as well as launching Hebrew exposure in the kindergarten and successive primary grades. The classical Reform movement had almost completely downplayed, if not virtually eliminated, Hebrew from the synagogue and the home. Since the late 1940s, Hebrew was being mainstreamed into new and old-line Reform congregations all across the country, except for Beth Israel.

Classical Reform, to its great credit, still vigorously championed the social-justice clarion call of the great Hebrew prophets of old as its signature mark of modern Jewish identity and religious challenge. Few of the old-line Reform congregations, however, back in the 1950s, made it a priority to establish formal social action committees encouraging members to move beyond the walls of the temple out into the larger community, which was forever crying out for compassionate help and volunteers to engage in desperately needed acts of human and community rebuilding. In my very first year at Beth Israel, we set in motion a brand-new temple social action committee that initiated an innovative inner-city tutorial program. This quickly managed to bring out a large and inspired wave of temple volunteers who in a very short time transformed the lives of legions of urban minority students at one of the city's poorest elementary schools.

As the years went by, the congregation moved actively into every conceivable area of community need, reaching out across all ethnic, racial, and religious lines. Nationally, since the mid-twentieth century, the entire American Reform movement has been a dynamic major player and leader among all religious groups in the United States, knee-deep in the commanding work of Tikkun Ha-Olam, repairing and rebuilding human lives and human society.

The national ferment among young people in the 1960s and 1970s made all of us in the Reform movement take a radical new look at the constructive and responsible role Jewish teenagers could and should be playing in the life of our congregations large and small. Despite some minor grumbling from the "old guard," pre-college teens in the temple were not only appointed to every important congregational committee, but most important, became voting members on the board of trustees, where their young and responsible voices were instrumental in helping to attune the older generation to the dynamic new winds of social and religious change blowing refreshingly through the "new" mainstream Reform.

Another vital area which was depressingly lacking in the worship area when I arrived in 1968 was the scheduling of monthly Friday-evening family-worship services, which had become the norm in nationwide Reform in the past two decades. While parents and children in the past had attended special children's services on the High Holy Days, Simchat

Torah, Hanukkah, and Purim, Friday nights at Beth Israel, for nearly a century, had been strictly scheduled for adults only. From 1970 on, we began to reach out to both generations, so that the whole family could enjoy periodic monthly worshipping together with a basically child-oriented liturgy. While we did manage to lose a small number of our regular adult Friday-evening service-goers, who looked upon the presence of children as a disturbing irritant in worship, the congregation at large benefited immeasurably from this new mainstream Reform family outreach, where the synagogue truly came to be looked upon as a multigenerational religious institution.

What I thought would really erupt into the crisis of crises was my recommendation in 1976 that our congregation adopt the newly revised Reform prayer book that had just been published by the Central Conference of American Reform rabbis. The last prayer book revision for our Reform movement had occurred in 1940, and was, in fact, a minimal revision of a pre-existing prayer book that went back in time to the World War I era of classical Reform. The old Reform prayer book was heavy on King James–type spiritual prose, a radical nontraditional right-to-left book opening, and bare-bones Hebrew-language content which was minimally spoken or even understood by the average lay worshipper.

I conducted several orientation sessions with the Sabbath evening cadre of temple worshippers to prepare them emotionally for the radically new structure and content of the movement's new prayer book, which was shortly to be placed in the pews. With all of my enthusiastic briefing in support of the new prayer book, I never really expected the transition and congregational acceptance to be as smooth and uncontroversial as happened. Notwithstanding some minor unhappiness and uncomfortableness registered by a pittance of the old-time classical German-background members, the majority of the East European newer members, along with a few open-minded German Jews, were quite pleased with the new liturgy.

To "sweeten the pot" for the more rigid old-timers, I promised in my orientation sessions to revisit the old *Union Prayer Book* periodically, never really intending to fulfill that risky promise. Fortunately, the new 1976 prayer book (called *Gates of Prayer*, as contrasted with the old *Union Prayer Book*) wisely included in its roster of multiple Sabbath evening services a clone-like religious service from the old book which I made certain to utilize frequently when the new book was introduced. Frankly, even the other brand-new services in *Gates of Prayer* were not that radically different or potentially jarring in relationship to the old book. Some of the new, more modern English prose, quite honestly, falls quite short, in my opinion, to the soaring and still elegant Victorian spiritual language and inspiration in the old *Union Prayer Book,* to which I always responded positively in my growing up at the Stephen Wise Synagogue in New York and in the early years of my rabbinate in Pittsburgh and in West Hartford.

An equally unexpected pleasant surprise awaited the Reform movement several years later in 1978 when most of our congregations were introduced to the radically new High Holy Day prayer book called *Gates of Repentance.* This once-a-year liturgy quickly won favor with rank-and-file congregants as well as with the dwindling number of German-Jewish classicists.

That very same decade of the 1970s also welcomed the long-overdue shelving of the old-line classical Reform Passover prayer book, *The Union Haggadah,* which had been around in several revised forms since 1920 and before. Many of our East European members, in joining Reform temples, frankly, had a difficult time warming up to the old *Union Haggadah,* which was a far, far cry from their pre-Reform days, when most of the Passover matzah companies in America provided free traditional-style Passover Haggadahs for the home service. The legendary Manischewitz paperback Haggadah, as if printed at Mount Sinai, was an old holiday staple across all movements in the United States. However, the new Reform Haggadah enjoyed the easiest entry and instant acceptance into Reform Jewish homes, thanks to its faithfulness to the authentic historical structure of the Passover Haggadah coupled with moving contemporary meditations reflecting the agonies of the Holocaust experience and the inclusion of modern-day Jewish writers from Albert Einstein to Anne Frank, along with breathtaking Passover images conceived by the brilliant and colorful artist Leonard Baskin. It too was published by the CCAR.

Another minor but telling shift away from the classical era of early Reform were my rabbinical moves to mainstream some of the ritual surrounding the wedding ceremony. This, too, had been going on in Reform congregations all across the country beginning in the late 1940s and the 1950s. For some reason, nineteenth- and early twentieth-century Reform rabbis had objected to the presence on the altar of the traditional wedding canopy, called the chuppah, under which Jewish brides and grooms historically stood, along with their parents, as well as the officiating rabbi, during the ceremony. The chuppah has for centuries symbolically represented the new home the couple was about to create in their married life. It was generally held up over the assembled immediate wedding party by four ushers. Many times the chuppah was an enlarged tallis, or prayer shawl. Sometimes, the shawl was held up by four standing poles. There were even times when a specially built chuppah-style "floral arch" was used. For some reason, the early Reform rabbis chose to do away with the chuppah, probably for no other reason than that in their minds it was deemed to be superfluously Orthodox.

In any event, many of the tradition-minded East European Jews joining Reform temples after the war retained warm memories of the chuppah and clung to it fondly as a still-meaningful and important Jewish symbol at Jewish weddings. They pressed their Reform rabbis to bring the chuppah back, and most of my postwar generation of Reform rabbis happily acceded.

The ritual of the shattering of the glass by the groom at the end of the wedding ceremony proved much tougher to deal with. Many pre–World War II classical Reform rabbis were troubled by two things that led them to do away with the glass-breaking wedding ritual. First and foremost, the early Reform rabbis objected to the pure and simple medieval aura of folk superstition bound up with the breaking of the glass. The centuries-old Jewish folk-belief was that the smashing of the glass was supposed to drive away the evil eye, or *ayin hara*, as it is known in Hebrew. The evil eye was long thought to hover dangerously around the wedding couple, not to mention the medieval fear of this same, ominous evil spirit hovering around every single Jewish life from the womb to the tomb. In the late nineteenth century, under the influence of modern enlightenment and intellectual integrity, the early reformers had no problem in dispensing with what they considered to be nothing more than a pagan and spiritually demeaning wedding superstition.

The classical Reform rabbis, however, had a far more substantive objection to the breaking of the glass than their mere aversion to superstition. Over the centuries, Orthodox rabbis went out of their way to interpret the shattered glass as a symbol connoting the destruction of the Second Temple by the Romans in the year 70 C.E. The homiletic explanation held that at the moment of a wedding couple's greatest happiness, they should not fail to recall this ancient national and religious calamity and pledge to do all in their power to sustain and enrich their people's group destiny in and out of the Holy Land.

The classical Reform rabbis of the late nineteenth and early twentieth centuries, however, no longer felt emotionally or historically attached to the Holy Land, looking upon America as the new Zion and true savior of the modern Jew. The growing Zionist movement in Europe and in the New World, they believed, threatened to focus the attention of American and world Jewry away from the messianic promise and fulfillment as to what the United States could messianically mean for modern Jewry. Many classical Reform rabbis and lay leaders in this period claimed that Zionist politics, particularly in the United States, were confronting American Jews with the potential charge of dual political allegiance, implying that one could not swear exclusive and total allegiance to America while working at the same time for Jewish nationalism in Palestine.

A small but vocal group of Reform rabbis and a claque of Reform laymen even went so far as to create, heavily finance, and promote an organization called the American Council for Judaism in the midst of World War II. This body proceeded to spew forth a bitter, unending media message of anti-Zionism with dire warnings to American Jews of their being accused of dual political allegiance. This kind of fevered anti-Zionism reached its peak during the post–World War II era leading up to the reestablishment of the Jewish state in May 1948.

While the council represented a bare minority of Reform rabbis and laity, it gave the false impression that a large percentage of American Jewry was disenchanted with and alarmed by the Zionist movement. In actual fact, the overwhelming majority of American Jewry, including postwar Reform Jewry, stood emotionally and politically foursquare behind the emergence of a Jewish state in Palestine, particularly in the light of the destruction of one-third of the Jewish people in Hitler's Europe and the urgent need for a secure and permanent homeland for the Jewish people.

Within several decades, the entire American Reform Jewish movement totally rejected the anti-Zionism of its classical founders. The Reform movement subsequently founded a national Reform Zionist organization called ARZA which inseparably bound the American Jewish Reform community emotionally and historically to the State of Israel.

Beginning in the 1970s, all entering Reform rabbinical students were required to spend the first year of the five-year post-graduate course of rabbinical studies in the Jerusalem branch of the Reform movement's rabbinical seminary. The "Year in Israel" program, which in time was also mandated for Reform cantors and educators, was probably the single greatest factor impelling a new generation of Reform rabbis to dramatically distance themselves from the movement's classical Jewish past.

Having to spend a whole year in Israel at the very beginning of their rabbinical studies proved, however, to be quite a shocker for the young Reform seminarians from America. The very first shock they had to absorb, particularly in Jerusalem, where they lived and studied, was the almost less than minority status Reform Judaism suffered in a city where Orthodox Judaism totally dominates the life and culture of the community. During the first fifty years of Israel's existence, Orthodoxy has had a virtual lock on Jerusalem's religious as well as civic life, to the point where vast numbers of non-Orthodox Israeli Jews were and still are unhappy enough to move out of Jerusalem to other parts of the country, where the heavy religious hand of Orthodoxy exerts little theological, legalistic, and social influence and a completely secular type of Jewishness prevails, as in Tel Aviv and Haifa.

Another great shock for the incipient Reform rabbis in their first year in the Israel program is the almost total ignorance of the history and practices of American Reform Judaism among the overwhelming majority of Israel's completely secular Jewish population, representing over 80 percent of the Israelis. The anti-religious sentiment over there, while anti-traditionalist in nature, is also motivated by Israelis wanting to be primarily defined by Jewish *national* citizenship and culture rather than being exclusively identified by historical Jewish religious status. In a word, most Israelis want to be Israelis and not necessarily Jews. They want their Judaism to be looked upon as a birthright "given"—something to be proud of, to be sure, but not to be mandated by suffocating ultra-right-wing rabbinical control.

What was and still is very hard for Reform rabbinical students to accept, and Reform Jewish tourists as well, is that for rank-and-file non-Orthodox Israelis, Orthodox Judaism, fanatical or even moderate, is the *only* style of Judaism they know or perhaps even want to know. Secular Israelis, sorrowfully, are completely in the dark about any other variety of or alternative to Orthodoxy. There are no required high school or college courses for Israeli students to learn about the denominational alternatives to Orthodoxy that abound in America and around the world. While a growing but tiny network of Reform and Conservative congregations exists today in Israel, non-Orthodox, American-style synagogue life remains but a minuscule blip on the religious radar screen of Israeli life.

As a result of the inferiority complex imposed upon them by scornful Orthodox Israelis and ignorant secular Israelis, the Reform rabbinical students have attempted over the years to don a traditional Orthodox image in the hope that nonstop wearing of yarmulkes, wearing the full tallis prayer shawl during worship, the sporting of beards, and the scrupulous observance of kashrut in their private Jerusalem home lives—that all of this will help them gain better acceptance among the Israeli Orthodox community. Unfortunately, the gulf over there between Orthodoxy and non-Orthodoxy remains as wide and as deep as ever.

When the rabbinical students complete their year in Israel and return to New York, Cincinnati, or Los Angeles to finish out the next four years of their seminary studies, they bring back with them a heightened feeling for traditional Orthodox practices and regimens which they consciously and unconsciously bring to their student pulpits in the United States. Upon ordination, as they begin their American pulpit careers, there is a natural, continuing openness and sensitivity toward wanting historically Reform congregations to be vastly more open to traditional Jewish rituals and life-styles. The students do not really want the Reform movement to become Orthodox. But they do want the American Reform movement to be vastly more accepting of the traditional Jewish past, which they fervently believe can, with creative revisions, enrich and deepen modern Reform Jewish lives. Hence the push in the present generation for far more Hebrew in the service, vastly more congregational participation, a more Torah-centered focus, the inclusion in the service of Jewish music and traditional cantorial cantillation, a substantially higher prioritizing of Sabbath observance in the home, and a richer and deeper observance of major and even minor Jewish holidays.

Mind you, I'm all for the "Year in Israel" program! I just believe that most Reform rabbinical students would be far better equipped to face the Orthodox Israeli scene, and Jewish life in general in the State of Israel, if they had several years of rabbinical studies in New York, Cincinnati, or Los Angeles under their belts. Let them still spend a full year in Israel, but in the third year of the five-year graduate studies, which would then initially ground them far more importantly in *American* Reform Jewish life before plunging directly, as babes in the wood, into the second- and third-class religious status and Reform Jewish defensiveness existing shamefully in the Jewish state. It was only after I had completed the entire rabbinical program in the New York School, where I was ordained in 1951, that I elected to spend half a year of post-seminary living and study in the infant State of Israel, where it was all pure inspiration that enabled me far better to cope with any and all Israeli Orthodox bias and brainwashing.

Half a century later, as we move now into the twenty-first century, large numbers of affiliated Reform Jews are still, unfortunately, confused and disoriented as to where our ever-changing mainstream Reform Judaism is heading. This was demonstrated vividly at the May 1999 convention of Reform rabbis in Pittsburgh. Over the past several years, the president of the Reform rabbinical organization, the Central Conference of American Rabbis, set in motion a process whereby, on the threshold of the twenty-first century, the Reform movement could come up with a new Statement of Principles that would more effectively and realistically guide Reform Jews and their congregations in the millennium ahead.

Twice before in the twentieth century (1937 and 1976) Reform rabbis strove to update and redefine some of the original late nineteenth-century theological, ceremonial, and historical social changes and new directions for the Reform movement. It was actually in Pittsburgh, way back in 1885, that the very first tiny group of Reform rabbis issued the movement's original landmark guidelines for Reform Judaism in this country. In 1885, as in 1937, Reform Judaism was dominated by German Jews. Its principles, by and large, reflected the totality and the weight of the German-Jewish response to unaccustomed religious freedom in Christian American society. The subsequent guidelines issued in 1976 and more recently during 1999 reflect a brand-new, almost totally East European constituency which has turned its back significantly upon a great deal of the classical German-Jewish past.

But not as much as one might imagine. Despite the unfortunately distorted local and national press coverage of the recent Statement of Principles voted upon by the Reform rabbis in Pittsburgh, the truth of the matter is that the so-called new "mainstream" Reform is closer to its classical past than its present-day East European constituency realizes. News coverage of Reform's new Statement of Principles, agreed upon by a large majority of the Reform rabbinate, gave the misleading headline impression that American Reform was turning *back* to Orthodoxy! Much was made of Reform rabbis and lay people now choosing to wear yarmulkes on their heads at worship, donning traditional prayer shawls around their shoulders, craving more Hebrew in the service, reacting warmly to cantorial chants in the liturgy, and experimenting with kosher foods at home. What was totally misleading in the reporting is that the main thrust of the new guidelines was not to champion a "return" to traditional ritual and ceremony. The guidelines only urged Reform Jews to be more receptive in their hearts, homes, and synagogues in considering how *some* historical Jewish practices can still, with a bit of creative modern adaptation, enrich and inspire the liberal religious lifestyle of today.

Rank-and-file Reform Jews today have a bigger problem with historical Reform. So many Reform Jews do not have the foggiest idea of Reform's original religious and philosophical past. To this day, they do not understand the gut reasons why the founding fathers of Reform in the nineteenth century radically broke away from Orthodox Judaism. Without minimizing the emotional appeal and present-day flirtation with certain Orthodox vestments and ceremonies by some Reform Jewish rabbis and congregants, which perhaps gives the "appearance" of a return to Orthodoxy, the alleged return overlooks the commanding "divide" between Reform and Orthodoxy, then and now, which has little or nothing to do with garb and diet. Without denigrating ritual one whit, the larger divide has always focused primarily on fundamental *doctrinal* matters of faith that are still at the very heart and core of our sectarian differences.

Reform Judaism, for example, continues to view the Mosaic laws in the Bible not as God-given but as legislation written by men who were inspired by God to mandate for humanity. Reform Judaism is still 180 degrees apart from Orthodoxy in maintaining that each new generation is not to be slavishly governed by rabbinic decisions of the past. What Reform still trumpets in this regard is that the observance or nonobservance of the laws and customs of the past must be contingent upon their spiritual and emotional relevancy for each new generation. Still another major shift away from

Orthodoxy is the basic core belief of Reform in the ultimate coming of a messianic *time* rather than in the coming of a messianic "person," where it remains our individual human responsibility and challenge to cause the messianic age to happen in *our* time. In yet another major departure from Orthodoxy, Reform also rejects outright the traditional Jewish belief in the physical resurrection of the dead, and places its emphasis on the hope for a *spiritual* resurrection of the soul where entrance into God's eternity is strictly contingent upon the quality of our moral and ethical life in the here-and-now.

Perhaps the greatest divide of all between Reform and Orthodoxy remains Reform's outright rejection of the insufferable second-class religious citizenship of women, who are still entrapped by traditional if not fanatical wagon-circling exclusion that makes a mockery of human egalitarianism.

Bad enough that the media, in general, are not astute enough to assess this deeper Reform-Orthodox divide and what it portends for the future. Worse still, in my mind, is the lamentable fact that a disturbingly large number of American Jews who proudly identify with the Reform movement haven't the foggiest idea why the doctrinal breakaway beliefs are still vital and germane. The divide between liberalism and traditionalism has little or nothing to do with ritual and ceremonial minutia. It will continue to focus primarily upon prime theological matters of faith which are still at the very heart and core of our sectarian differences, and these, frankly, will *never* be bridged.

What should matter first and foremost in the eyes, hearts, and minds of better-educated and truly perceptive modern Reform Jews is the mature and larger recognition that there is, to be sure, a "return" going on in the Reform movement. But the return is a natural and inevitable return to our collective religious senses, and as such it is enabling us liberal Jews to do full justice to the best of our entire past where that past still has so much to inspire the present. As we move into the twenty-first century, I am totally convinced that in the generations ahead we can still follow the dynamic lead of the great Hebrew prophets of old, who faced the same great religious challenge in their age as do Reform Jews today: to create a crucial *balance* between ritual and ethics where each remains an indispensable and continuing proud hallmark of the Jewish faith and spells out what it essentially means to be Jewish.